Pupil Book 6

Written by Jayne Campling, Andrew Jeffrey,
Adella Osborne and Dr Tony Wing

OXFORD

Contents

How to use this book

Welcome to Numicon Pupil Book 6.

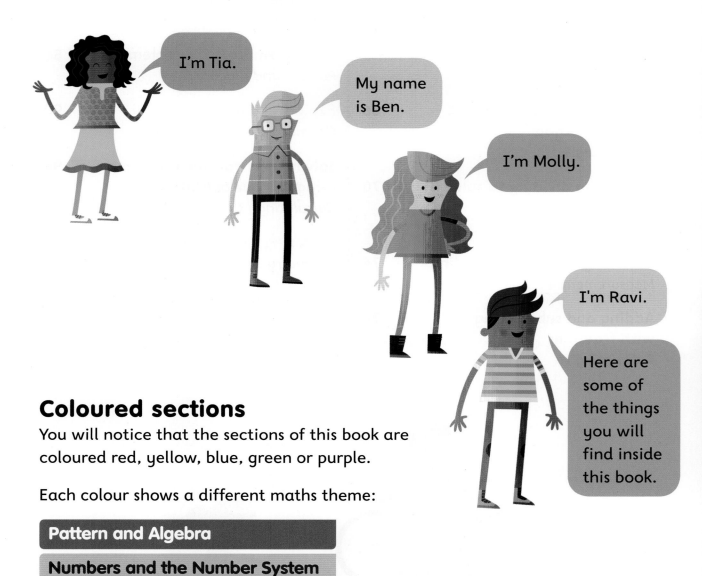

I'm Tia.

My name is Ben.

I'm Molly.

I'm Ravi.

Here are some of the things you will find inside this book.

Coloured sections

You will notice that the sections of this book are coloured red, yellow, blue, green or purple.

Each colour shows a different maths theme:

Pattern and Algebra

Numbers and the Number System

Calculating

Geometry

Measurement

In this book you can try out new calculations...

... and new methods for finding answers.

There are opportunities to look for patterns...

...and to think about how different maths ideas are connected.

Practice

These questions help you to practise and explore the new maths ideas you have learned.

Going deeper

These questions give you extra challenge and make you think deeply.

You will need to work with a partner on questions that have this symbol.

When you see this grey symbol you can do these activities in the Explorer Progress Book.

Glossary

There is a glossary of maths words in the back of the book. In the glossary you can look up the meaning of words you don't know.

Exploring large numbers

Norway population:
5 223 256

Switzerland
population: 8 341 600

More people live
in Switzerland
than in Norway.

Molly

Ben

Practice

 1 a Can you say both Molly's and Ben's numbers to your partner?

b Is Ben correct? Explain to a partner how you know.

c What is the value of the '3' in each of the numbers?

2 a Which of these countries' populations is the greatest?

Seychelles 91 437	Hong Kong (China) 7 234 400	Luxembourg 576 300
Sierra Leone 7 085 631	Hungary 9 823 070	Serbia 8 778 826

 b Can you order the populations from the greatest to the least? Compare your answers with a partner's.

3 What is the value of each '7' in the populations above? Can you explain how you work out these values?

Going deeper

1 Can you write the number that is 10 000 more than 91 400?

2 Can you write down the numbers between 9 531 712 and 9 611 712, leaving 10 000 between each number?

Looking at the value of digits in large numbers

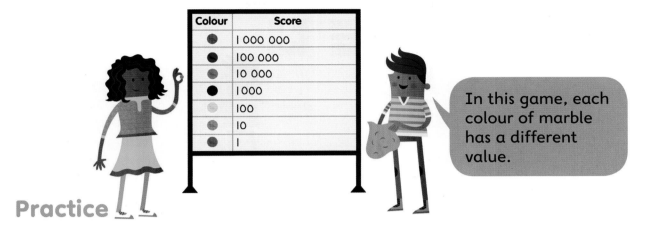

In this game, each colour of marble has a different value.

Practice

1 Ravi pulls out the marbles below. What number has he scored?

2 Tia pulls out the marbles below and says her number is 113 142, but she is not correct. Can you explain why not and give the correct answer?

3 Ravi and Tia play again and this time they each take 20 marbles out.

   a How many of each colour of marble does Ravi need to pull out to make the number 3 045 602?

   b Can you find six different combinations of 20 marbles that would beat Ravi's score and use more than one colour of each marble?

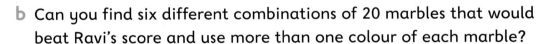

Going deeper

1 If there are ten of each kind of marble in the bag:

   a what is the biggest multiple of 5 you can make using ten marbles

   b what is the smallest multiple of 3 you can make using ten marbles?

2 Can you make a number that has no thousands or hundreds using ten marbles?

3 Tia pulls out ten marbles. She pulls out twice as many yellow marbles as green marbles and twice as many green marbles as orange marbles. She pulls out three blue marbles. What number must she have?

Rounding large numbers

Norway population:
5 223 256

Switzerland population:
8 341 600

The population in Switzerland rounded to the nearest 100 000 is 8 300 000.

Practice

1 What is the population of Norway rounded to the nearest 100 000? Explain to a partner how you know.

2 Can you copy this number line and mark approximately where the number 5 223 256 will appear?

5 200 000   5 300 000

3 Can you round the population of Norway to the nearest:

   a 10 000   b 1000

   c 100   d 10?

4 Sierra Leone has a population of approximately 7 085 631. What is this rounded to the nearest:

   a 1 000 000   b 100 000   c 10 000

   d 1000   e 100   f 10?

....

Going deeper

1 Can you list five numbers that will round up to 3 340 000 to the nearest 10 000?

2 Can you write a number that would round to 1 100 000 to the nearest 100 000 and 1 062 000 to the nearest 1000?

 3 Hayley is thinking of a number. When it is rounded to the nearest ten thousand it is 1 280 000. Can you work out the range of numbers her number must fall into? Discuss with a partner.

 4

Exploring the values of digits in decimal numbers

Practice

 1 a Can you explain why this statement is true?

    b What is the value of the 3, the 2 and the 5?

2 Can you write each pair of numbers below with either a > or < sign between the numbers to make the statements correct?

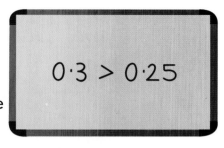

0·3 > 0·25

    a 1·8   1·65   b 0·503   0·65   c 2·067   2·12

3 Can you write a number with three decimal places that is bigger than 0·5 but less than 0·75?

Going deeper

1 Can you list three numbers that lie between 1·45 and 1·46?

2 Ellie is thinking of a number with three decimal places. Its hundredths digit is twice its tenths digit and the thousandths digit is three times the tenths digit.
The number is less than 0·25.
Which **two** possible numbers could Ellie be thinking of?

 3 Can you create some similar 'thinking of a number' questions to give to a partner to solve?

 4 Try this game with a partner.

- Take it in turns to write a 7-digit number down, keeping it hidden.

- Give your partner clues, including two rounding clues.

- Keep giving clues until your partner guesses correctly.

Using negative numbers

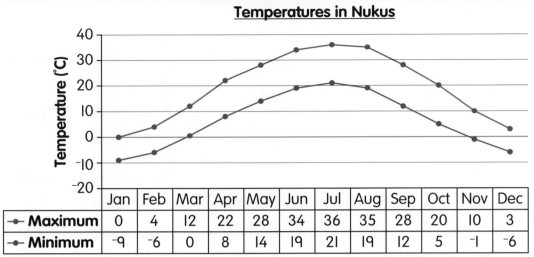

Temperatures in Nukus

	Jan	Feb	Mar	Apr	May	Jun	Jul	Aug	Sep	Oct	Nov	Dec
Maximum	0	4	12	22	28	34	36	35	28	20	10	3
Minimum	⁻9	⁻6	0	8	14	19	21	19	12	5	⁻1	⁻6

Practice

1 Jack has found a graph showing the monthly maximum and minimum temperatures in Nukus, Uzbekistan.

   a In which months does the temperature **sometimes** fall below freezing?

   b Which is the coldest month?

   c Which months are generally hotter than the month of May?

2 Which months have the same minimum temperature?

....

Going deeper

1 Can you copy and complete the sentences below with 'colder' or 'warmer'?

   a ⁻10°C is _____ than ⁻5°C   b 15°C is _____ than ⁻20°C

   c ⁻12°C is _____ than ⁻18°C

2 Can you give a whole number that is between:

   a ⁻9 and ⁻6   b ⁻6 and 4?

3 Can you suggest a temperature for each missing box to keep the temperatures in order from coldest to warmest?

   ▮°C   ⁻50°C   ▮°C   ⁻15°C   ▮°C   1°C   18°C

Finding differences

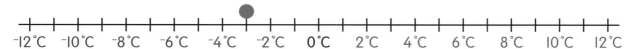

Masha places her counter on ⁻3°C. She turns over a card and has to move her counter to follow the instruction.

Practice

1 What number will Masha's counter be on after she has followed the instruction on the card to the right? | 2°C fall |

2 Next, Masha turns over these three cards:

| 9°C rise | | 15°C fall | and | 4°C rise |

Where will her counter be after she has completed all three moves?

3 Can you work out the difference between:

a 0°C and ⁻9°C   b 4°C and ⁻6°C   c ⁻1°C and 10°C?

....

Going deeper

1 a Hazel recorded the temperature at night as a whole number. It was colder than 0°C, but warmer than ⁻4°C. Can you list the temperatures it could have been?

   b Can you think of a temperature and then give clues to help your partner work out what it is?

2 Can you give three pairs of temperatures (one positive and one negative) that have a difference of 12°C?

3 Can you explain how we can use a number line to show infinite pairs of temperatures with the same difference?

Profit and loss

Bill runs an ice cream shop. It costs Bill £1 for each ice cream. He sells each ice cream for £1·80.

Ice cream
£1·80

The running costs for the shop are £50 a day. Bill records the number of ice creams sold each day in this table.

Day	Ice cream sales	Total money taken
Monday	30	£54
Tuesday	10	£18
Wednesday	50	£90
Thursday	70	£126
Friday	60	£108
Saturday	120	£216
Sunday	140	£252

Practice

1 On which days does the ice cream shop make a loss?

2 Can you calculate the profit or loss for each day? Give your answers for each day in negative or positive amounts.

3 An ice cream company makes £25 000 one month but its costs were £40 000. How much of a loss did it make that month?

Going deeper

1 Look at the table above. The next week, sales at the shop were halved due to bad weather. Can you work out the profit or loss for each day? Give each answer as a negative or positive amount.

2 Can you make up four calculations that will give you an answer of ⁻£650?

3 Work with your partner to turn your calculations from **question 2** into word problems.

Adding and subtracting large numbers

The picture shows how much luggage each aeroplane can hold and how much the luggage weighs on a flight.

a

Capacity of 18 000 kg

Luggage weight 15 762 kg

b

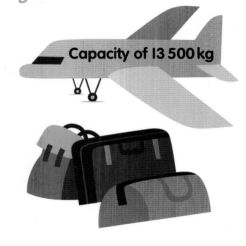

Capacity of 13 500 kg

Luggage weight 9050 kg

Practice

1 Can you calculate how much extra luggage each plane could still hold? Discuss and agree your method. Can you think of other methods?

2 Can you calculate 12 564 − 8395? What do you think is the best method for this calculation? Can you explain why?

3 Can you solve 18 635 + ▮ = 254 729? What do you think is the best method for this calculation? Can you explain why?

Going deeper

1 Without calculating the answer to each subtraction, can you solve these problems?

a 18 000 − 15 762 = 16 500 − ▮   b 13 500 − 9050 = ▮ − 10 000

c Can you explain your thinking?

2 Copy and complete this table.

3 Can you create your own table puzzle for a partner to solve?

+	16 472	?
?	56 423	?
46 284	?	64 732

Multiplying using factors

25 seats in a row

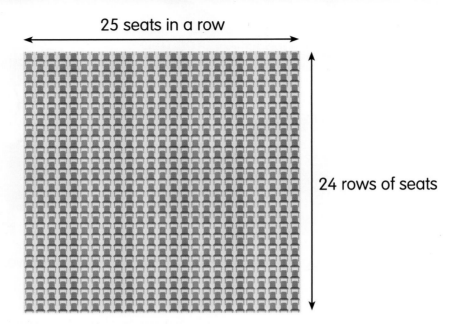

24 rows of seats

A football stadium has 24 rows of 25 seats.

Practice

 1 How many seats does the football stadium have altogether? Can you use factors of 24 or 25 to simplify the calculation 24 × 25? Share and compare your strategy with your partner.

2 Using factors can you calculate:

   a 15 × 36   b 18 × 25   c 120 × 42?

··

Going deeper

1 The 6-key is broken on a calculator. How could you use this calculator to work out 46 × 16? Make a record of which keys you would press on the calculator.

 2 If you know the answer to 24 × 25, how could you work out 12 × 50? Can you explain your thinking?

3 Using factors, what do you think is the best way to calculate 175 × 28?

Multiplying using partitioning

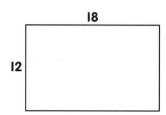

Neema is calculating 18 × 12 and is using this diagram to help her.

Practice

1 How might you split up the rectangle to simplify Neema's calculation? Now solve it and use a drawing to show your thinking.

2 Using the same approach, can you solve these multiplying calculations by partitioning?

   a 15 × 32   b 52 × 45   c 38 × 19

 3 Compare your methods with a partner for working out the answers to question 2. Can you split the calculations up in any other way?

Going deeper

1 How could you simplify and solve 180 × 12?

2 Using a rectangle 25 × 64, can you find five different ways of splitting the rectangle to calculate its area?

 3 Take it in turns to turn over two numeral cards from a 1–99 pack. Write the multiplying sentence and then try to beat your partner to the answer by using a method that simplifies the calculation.

Partitioning and dividing

64 ÷ 4 is the same as 32 ÷ 2.

150 ÷ 6 is the same as 50 ÷ 2.

Practice

 1 Can you explain why both Tia and Ben are correct?

2 Can you solve these dividing calculations by making them simpler first?

   a 300 ÷ 6   **b** 848 ÷ 16   **c** 540 ÷ 9

3 Can you find two different ways of calculating 160 ÷ 32?

Going deeper

 1 Can you find another way to work out 150 ÷ 6 using common factors? Explain your strategy to a partner.

2 Can you simplify $\frac{192}{12}$ and write four different dividing calculations that give the same quotient?

 3 How might you solve 342 ÷ 18? Discuss your reasons with your partner.

Multiplying and dividing by 10, 100 and 1000

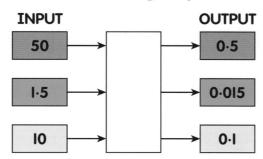

Christopher puts some numbers into a function machine.

Practice

 1 What function must be inside the machine? Can you explain how you worked this out?

2 Can you put three more numbers into the function machine and then give the new numbers that would come out?

3 Can you multiply these numbers by 1000?

   a 6·4   b 10·75   c 140·8

4 How many times larger is 12 500 than 12·5?

5 How many times smaller is 1·05 than 105?

Going deeper

 1 Play this game with a partner:

   • write down a number

   • your partner then secretly multiplies or divides the number by 10, 100 or 1000 and passes the answer to you

   • work out what their calculation must have been and write it down.

2 Can you give a number that, when divided by 1000, lies between 0·1 and 0·2?

Introducing the mean (average)

Tia   Molly   Ravi   Ben

Practice

1 The children have just had their test papers marked and returned to them. Can you explain how to find their mean score?

2 Two of the children realize that the mean score of their two tests is 49%. Can you work out which two?

3 One child wants to take the test again and their score is taken out of the mean. The mean is now 58%. Can you work out which child decided to take the test again?

....

Going deeper

1 To qualify for the final of a 100m race, Jonah needs to do three runs with a mean time of less than 11 seconds. His first two runs take 10·4 and 11·2 seconds respectively. How fast must Jonah run his third run in order to qualify?

   Can you explain how you worked this out?

2 Andrew is counting how many times he can skip in one minute. After his first five attempts his mean number of skips is 62. After one more attempt this goes up slightly to 64. How many skips did he manage on his sixth attempt?

Using the mean

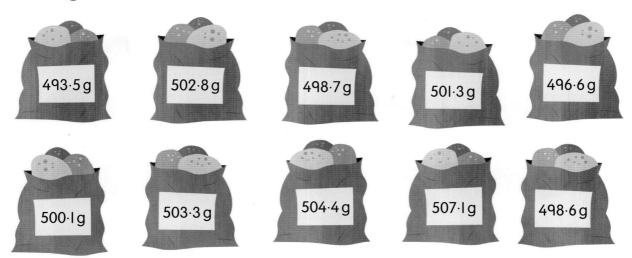

Practice

1 Samara is checking the weight of these ten bags of potatoes to ensure that they meet the regulations.

   a Samara has been told to reject any bags that are more than 1% lighter than the mean mass. Which bags she should reject?

   b Do you think it would be fair to label the bags 'Half Kilo' bags? Can you explain your thinking?

....

Going deeper

1 Samara is asked to check the volume of liquid in some drinks cartons that claim to hold 330 ml. From a sample of four cartons, she is pleased to find that the mean average is exactly 330 ml. The first three cartons she tests contain 331·1 ml, 327·2 ml and 329·4 ml. Can you find the volume of liquid in the fourth carton?

2 Tim, aged 40, joins a band and becomes its fifth member. He raises the mean average age of the band members to 36. Can you work out what the average age was before Tim joined?

Average speeds and units of speed

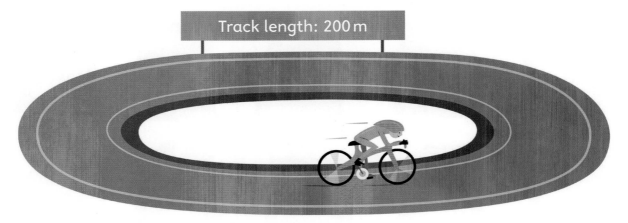

Track length: 200 m

Practice

1 Bradley is cycling around this track at a velodrome. After 10 minutes he has completed exactly 30 laps. What is his average speed in km/h?

2 Draw axes with time up to 1 hour on the x-axis, and distance up to 40 km on the y-axis. Using your answer from question 1, can you draw a line to show Bradley's average speed?

3 Can you use the graph to find out how far Bradley could cycle in 20 minutes?

4 Now try using your graph to find out how long Bradley would take to cycle 75 laps.

Going deeper

1 Candice drives on the motorway for half an hour, at an average speed of 90 km/h. She then drives through some roadworks and has to slow down to an average speed of 60 km/h. If she spends a quarter of an hour driving through the roadworks, how long does Candice's journey take altogether and how far has she driven?

2 Nadia and Zane are having a 10-mile race. Nadia runs at an average speed of 5 mph, and Zane runs at an average speed of 9 km/h. Who wins, and by approximately how much time? Talk to a partner about how you worked this out.

Constructing and interpreting pie charts

Practice

The children are playing a game. They have to throw as many balls into their bucket as they can.

Ravi got 2 balls in.　　Ben got 8 balls in.　　Molly got 8 balls in.　　Tia got 18 balls in.

1 a Draw a bar chart and a pie chart to show how many balls are in each bucket.

b Which chart do you think is more useful? Can you explain why?

 2 Which chart is most useful for answering each question below?

a What fraction of the balls is in Tia's bucket?

b What is the difference between the number of balls in Ravi's bucket and the number of balls in Tia's bucket?

Going deeper

1 a A designer asks people what colour dresses they prefer. Use the information to complete the table.

Twice as many people said 'red' as 'blue'. Half the people said either 'white' or 'red'.
The number of people who said 'blue' was double the number who said 'yellow'.

Black	White	Blue	Yellow	Green	Red
25%	?	?	?	?	20%

b Now choose a diagram to draw which will show this data in a useful way.

c If the designer makes 200 dresses, how many should be green?

Exploring factors and multiples

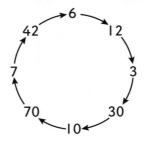

Practice

1 Can you describe how this circular number chain has been made?

2 Can you make a similar circular chain for yourself, starting with any whole number in the range 1–10, without repeating any numbers?

3 What is the longest circular number chain like these that you can make? How do your choices affect the length of the chain?

4 How many different factor trees, like those below, can you make beginning with 80?

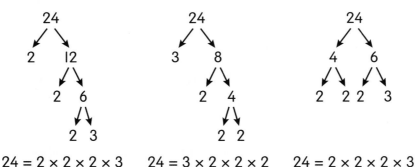

$$24 = 2 \times 2 \times 2 \times 3 \qquad 24 = 3 \times 2 \times 2 \times 2 \qquad 24 = 2 \times 2 \times 2 \times 3$$

Going deeper

1 Can you make a circular number chain using the numbers 5, 6, 9, 30, 45 and 54?

2 Can you explain why circular number chains make circles?

3 Can you explain a good strategy for creating factor trees? Illustrate your strategy by making a factor tree for the number 224.

Using factors when multiplying and dividing

This diagram shows 180 ÷ 12 = 180 ÷ 3 ÷ 4.

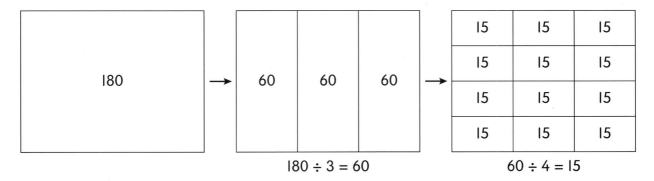

180 ÷ 3 = 60   60 ÷ 4 = 15

Practice

1 Can you draw a diagram like the one above to show that 225 ÷ 15
  = 225 ÷ 3 ÷ 5?

2 Rewrite the calculations below in as many different ways as you can.
  Can you choose which versions you think would be the easiest to use to
  calculate the answer?

  a 16 × 24   b 504 ÷ 24   c 198 ÷ 18   d 25 × 15

3 Can you rewrite the calculations below as fractions, and then
  simplify them?

  a 300 ÷ 18   b 252 ÷ 21

Going deeper

1 How many different ways can you find to calculate each of the following?

  a 23 × 15   b 16 × 36   c 28 × 13   d 19 × 17

2 Which calculation in **question 1** did you find the hardest and why?

3 How might knowing the prime factors of 720 help you to calculate
  720 ÷ 16? Can you explain why?

Using the lowest common multiple (LCM)

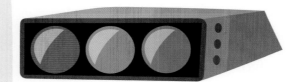

Disco light instructions:
- Press start.
- The red light will flash every 10 seconds.
- The blue light will flash every 14 seconds.
- The green light will flash every 25 seconds.

Practice

1 Can you work out when all three lights will first flash together? Give your answer in seconds.

2 Choose two whole numbers between 2 and 12, and find all their common multiples in the range 50–150. Can you find their LCM?

3 Which numbers in this list are common multiples of smaller numbers?

> 24   39   60   84   74   48   54   30

Can you say which smaller numbers these are common multiples of?

.....

Going deeper

1 Using their prime factors, can you draw a Venn diagram to help you work out the LCM of 8 and 30?

2 This Venn diagram shows the prime factors of two numbers. Can you say what the two numbers are, and name their LCM?

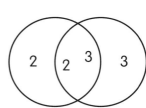

3 How could you have used a Venn diagram to help you solve the disco lights problem above?

Exploring highest common factors (HCF)

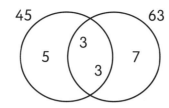

The HCF of 45 and 63 is 3 × 3 = 9.

Practice

1 Can you use a Venn diagram to calculate the HCF of these numbers?

   a 56 and 96   b 72 and 90   c 81 and 27

2 Without using the number '7' itself, can you find five pairs of numbers that have an HCF of 7?

3 How many different pairs of numbers can you find between 50 and 100 that have an HCF of 6?

Going deeper

1 Can you work out the largest possible HCF of a pair of whole numbers up to and including 100?

2 Can you work out the answer to **question 1** again, but this time the smaller number of the pair cannot be a factor of the larger number?

3 Can you list all the number pairs within the range 50–100 whose only common factor is 7? How do you know you have found them all?

Exploring fractions

All these fractions are greater than $\frac{1}{2}$.

$$\frac{3}{4} \quad \frac{3}{8} \quad \frac{7}{10} \quad \frac{4}{5} \quad \frac{9}{16}$$

Practice

1 Can you explain to a partner whether Ben is correct or not?

2 Can you order the fractions above from smallest to largest? You can use apparatus to support you.

3 Can you suggest three more fractions that are greater than $\frac{1}{2}$?

4 Can you order the fractions in each group below from smallest to largest?

a $\frac{2}{3}$ $\frac{7}{9}$ $\frac{1}{2}$ $\frac{1}{6}$ $\frac{1}{4}$ b $\frac{5}{12}$ $\frac{1}{3}$ $\frac{5}{6}$ $\frac{1}{8}$ $\frac{5}{24}$ c $\frac{3}{7}$ $\frac{1}{4}$ $\frac{3}{14}$ $\frac{5}{7}$ $\frac{1}{2}$

Going deeper

1 Which of Ben's fractions above are bigger than $\frac{3}{4}$? Can you explain how you know?

2 Can you write five proper fractions in order from smallest to largest using numbers from the lists below? You can only use each number once. Compare your fractions with a partner. Can you agree a definition for a proper fraction?

Numerators
1 5 9 3 6

Denominators
9 15 12 8 6

3 Take turns to give your partner a proper fraction, for example $\frac{2}{3}$. Your partner must give you a smaller proper fraction that has a different denominator, for example $\frac{1}{6}$. Record your answers in this way: $\frac{2}{3} > \frac{1}{6}$.

Converting and comparing fractions

I got $\frac{3}{4}$ of the 20 questions correct in the spelling test.

I scored 17 out of 20 in the spelling test.

Molly

Ravi

Tia

I got $\frac{2}{3}$ of the 30 questions correct in the maths test.

I scored 18 out of 30 in the maths test.

Ben

Practice

1 a Who scored the higher mark in the spelling test? How do you know?

   b Who scored the higher mark in the maths test? How do you know?

2 Another child gained a spelling test mark that was between Molly's and Ravi's. What mark did they score, out of 20?

3 Another child got $\frac{5}{6}$ of the maths test correct. What do you think their score was?

 4 What is the common denominator for each group of fractions below? List the fractions with their new denominator.

   a $\frac{3}{8}$ $\frac{1}{6}$ $\frac{5}{12}$ $\frac{1}{3}$ b $\frac{7}{10}$ $\frac{5}{8}$ $\frac{3}{4}$ $\frac{3}{5}$ c $\frac{7}{9}$ $\frac{5}{6}$ $\frac{2}{3}$ $\frac{7}{12}$

Going deeper

1 Can you order these fractions, starting with the smallest? $\frac{3}{4}$ $\frac{17}{20}$ $\frac{2}{3}$ $\frac{18}{30}$

2 Can you name two fractions which lie between:

   a $\frac{1}{6}$ and $\frac{2}{5}$ b $\frac{1}{3}$ and $\frac{3}{7}$?

3 Can you name five proper fractions that are greater than $\frac{4}{5}$? Can you explain your strategy for finding these fractions?

Simplifying fractions

Tia and Ben
are interested
in which scores
occur most
often when they
throw two dice
and record the
total. They throw
the two dice 80
times.

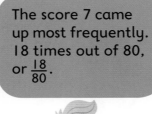

The score 7 came up most frequently. 18 times out of 80, or $\frac{18}{80}$.

Score	Frequency
2	2
3	4
4	6
5	8
6	11
7	18
8	12
9	10
10	5
11	3
12	1

Practice

 1 Can you simplify the fraction $\frac{18}{80}$? How could you explain what 'simplifying' a fraction means to your partner?

 2 Can you write and simplify the fractions for the other scores in the table? Are there some that cannot be simplified? Can you explain why not?

3 Can you simplify these fractions?

   a $\frac{5}{40}$ b $\frac{3}{27}$ c $\frac{16}{56}$ d $\frac{48}{72}$

4 Can you name three fractions that would all simplify to $\frac{2}{5}$? What is a good method for finding these?

Going deeper

 1 Write five fractions that can be simplified for your partner to simplify. What makes some fractions more difficult to simplify than others?

 2 "To simplify fractions, halve the numerator and denominator until you can't do it any more." Is this statement sometimes, always or never true? Can you explain your thinking?

Ordering mixed numbers

Four children are completing a sponsored relay by doing laps of their school field.

Name	Laps completed
Jamie	$4\frac{3}{4}$
Raj	$3\frac{1}{2}$
Louise	$3\frac{2}{3}$
Vanessa	$4\frac{5}{6}$

Practice

1 Who ran the furthest? Can you explain your thinking?

2 Can you order all the mixed numbers above, showing the smallest number of laps first?

3 Can you order the mixed numbers below from smallest to largest?

   a $1\frac{3}{8}$ $1\frac{2}{5}$ $2\frac{3}{10}$ $2\frac{1}{4}$ b $1\frac{2}{9}$ $1\frac{1}{6}$ $2\frac{1}{4}$ $2\frac{5}{12}$

 4 Can you name a mixed number that would lie between $1\frac{1}{4}$ and $1\frac{1}{3}$? How did you choose this, and how do you know you are correct?

....

Going deeper

1 Can you write one mixed number that would lie between each pair of results in the ordered set of relay results from question 2?

2 Can you write three mixed numbers that would lie between $2\frac{1}{2}$ and $2\frac{3}{4}$?

 3 Take it in turns to think of a mixed number and then give clues to help your partner guess what it is.

Estimating and rounding

Country	Car production numbers 2015
Germany	6 033 164
Japan	9 278 238
UK	1 682 156
France	1 970 000
Spain	2 733 210
Italy	1 014 223
India	4 125 744

0   10 000 000

Practice

1 a Can you round each of the car production numbers to the nearest 10 000?

   b Draw a number line like the one above. Can you place the countries in order along your line?

2 Can you round each of the car production numbers to:

   a the nearest 100 000   b the nearest 1000   c the nearest 100?

Going deeper

1 Which country do you think makes roughly twice as many cars as France?

2 If Italy's car production were to increase by 10%, how many extra cars would this be, to the nearest 1000?

3 If 1% of the cars produced in Japan were sold to the UK, how many cars would this be, to the nearest 100?

Estimating quantities and costs

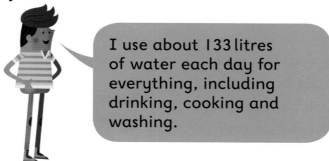

I use about 133 litres of water each day for everything, including drinking, cooking and washing.

Practice

1 As there are 365 days in a year, Ravi estimates that he will therefore use roughly 40 000 litres of water each year. He does this by rounding 133 and 365 to the nearest hundred, giving 100 × 400 = 40 000. Can you make a closer estimate than Ravi's?

2 Assume that everyone uses the same amount of water as Ravi and that there are on average 2·3 people in every household. Molly estimates that one household uses 2 × 50 000 = 100 000 litres of water each year. Can you explain how she estimated?
Can you make a closer estimate than Molly's?

3 1000 litres (or 1 cubic metre) of water costs £1·948. Molly estimates that water will cost an average household roughly £200 each year. Do you think Molly's estimate will be higher or lower than the actual cost? Can you explain why?

Going deeper

1 Assume that the average amount of water that one person uses annually is 133 × 365 = 48 545 litres. Rounding each figure to the nearest 100 gives 40 000 litres, but rounding each figure to the nearest 10 gives 130 × 370 = 48 100 litres. Can you explain why rounding both figures to the nearest 10 is so much more accurate?

2 Edinburgh, in Scotland, had 230 831 households in 2015. Can you estimate how many cubic metres of water Edinburgh used in one day in 2015? Explain how you made your estimate. Do you think your estimate will be higher or lower than the actual amount used?

Rounding

Practice

1 a Flour comes in bags of 1·4 kg. Can you work out how many bags of flour will be needed to make 300 cheese straws?

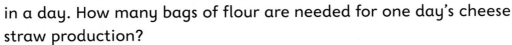

Recipe for 15 cheese straws

350 g flour
225 g butter
150 g cheddar cheese
2 eggs
$\frac{1}{4}$ teaspoon salt

b The cheese straws are sold in packs of 8 and the bakers are planning to make 100 packs in a day. How many bags of flour are needed for one day's cheese straw production?

c At the end of a day's production, the bakers want to use up all the flour they bought. How many extra packs of cheese straws can they make?

Going deeper

1 Can you write a 7-digit number that gives the same number when rounded to either the nearest 10 000 or to the nearest 100 000?

2 The children each have one of these cards.

| 425 129 | 420 356 | 399 874 | 399 996 |

Can you work out who has which card?

My number has exactly 3998 hundreds in it.

My number is 420 000 to the nearest 10 000.

My number is 400 000 to the nearest 100 000.

My number is 400 000 to the nearest 10.

Molly

Ravi

Ben

Tia

Estimating answers to calculations

Practice

1 Using any of Molly's numbers once only, and any of the operations
+, −, × or ÷, how close can you get to the answers below?

a 274   **b** 256   **c** 732   **d** 598   **e** 412

2 Explain how you would estimate answers to each of these calculations.
Do you think each estimate will be higher or lower than the actual
answer?

a 659 + 328   **b** 123 × 4·8   **c** 1472 − 748   **d** 270 ÷ 8·7

e 324 + 573   **f** 8·9 × 21·5   **g** 3347 − 419   **h** 62·7 ÷ 6·8

Going deeper

1 Think about the calculation 9·3 × 138·8. If you can only round **one** of
the decimal numbers to the nearest whole number, which one would
you round to get closest to the actual answer? Can you explain why?

2 A country made 5·1 million cars in 2014 (to the nearest hundred
thousand), compared with 5 million cars (to the nearest million) in 2013.
Sanjay thinks that they made more cars in 2014 than in 2013. Is he
correct, do you think? Can you explain why?

3 Using **all** of the numbers 75, 25, 2, 7, 4 and 8 **once** each, and any of the
operations +, −, × or ÷, how close can you get to each of these answers:

a 348   **b** 504   **c** 769   **d** 230?

Exploring column methods for adding

 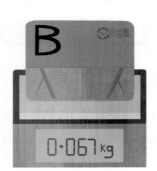 

A 0·158 kg   B 0·067 kg   C 0·193 kg

Practice

1 a Tia wants to post parcel A and parcel B. Can you estimate the combined mass of the parcels? Now calculate the answer exactly using the written column method. How close were you?

   b Can you estimate and then calculate how much parcel B and parcel C weigh altogether? How close were you this time?

   c Estimate and then calculate how much parcel A and parcel C weigh altogether. How close were you? Are you getting better at estimating?

2 If Tia ties a length of string around each parcel, adding 0·007 kg to each weight above, how much will each parcel weigh now?

Going deeper

 1 Can you add the masses below by estimating first and then calculating using the written column method? Discuss your strategies with a partner.

   a 0·28 kg and 0·817 kg   b 0·704 kg and 0·097 kg   c 0·345 kg and 0·886 kg

2 Tia wraps parcel D which weighs 0·275 kg. Which parcels A–D would give a combined mass of no more than $\frac{1}{2}$ kg? List the masses of the different combinations in order of size.

3 Choose one of your combination calculations from above and check your adding by doing some subtracting.

Working out change by subtracting

£3·75 per kg

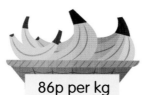
86p per kg

£2·69 per kg

£2·24 per kg

Practice

1 a Ben buys a kilogram of melons and a kilogram of bananas. How much money will he have left?

   b Ravi buys a kilogram of lemons and a kilogram of pears. How much money will he have left?

2 Can you use a written column method to calculate:

   a 9·67 – 2·38   b 10·05 – 7·14

   c 8·1 – 5·65   d 6·11 – 3·74?

Now use the inverse to check that your answers are correct.

Ben's Money £8·45

Ravi's Money £10·24

Going deeper

1 Look at the money Ben and Ravi start with above. Do they each have enough money to buy a kilogram of each fruit? How much money is left over or how much more do they need?

 2 Looking at the calculations below, can you work out what has gone wrong? Discuss what you think has happened with a partner. Complete the correct calculation for each.

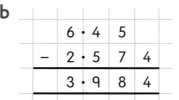

a

	8	·	0	6	8
–	3	·	4	7	4
	5	·	1		4

b

	6	·	4	5	
–	2	·	5	7	4
	3	·	9	8	4

c

	5	·	0	0	7
–	3	·	1	2	9
	1	·	9	8	8

3 Can you find two different subtracting calculations that will give the answer 2·547?

31

Subtracting using equal adding

Lily is working out 456 – 168. This is the method she is using.

	4	¹5	¹6
–	²1̶	⁷6̶	8
	2	8	8

Practice

 1 Can you explain Lily's method to your partner?

2 Using the same method as Lily, can you work out:

   a 864 – 238   b 542 – 185

   c 15·65 – 9·73   d 12·04 – 7·46?

 3 Can you solve each of these empty box problems, without doing the subtracting calculation on the left?

   a 673 – 134 = 675 – ■   b 1002 – 875 = ■ – 873

   c 4·6 – 1·25 = ■ – 1·5   d 12·5 – 7·7 = 15 – ■

   Compare your answers with your partner and explain your thinking.

··

Going deeper

1 Can you write a similar equal adding calculation to Lily's above that requires:

   a adding 10 to each number

   b adding 10 to each number and then 100 to each number?

 2 Can you each create four balancing calculations like the ones in question 3 for your partner to solve? Discuss and agree your answers by explaining your methods to each other.

Missing number problems

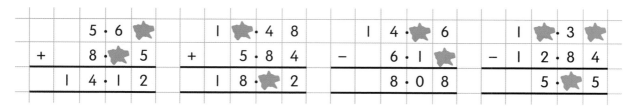

Ali spilled his drink and smudged some of the numbers in his book.

Practice

1 Can you work out what missing digits are hidden by the splodges for each calculation? Check by completing the calculations.

2 a Choose one number from each list to create an adding calculation. Do this three times with different number pairs.

> **A:** 56·8 32·43 16·126 11·73 0·562 125·67

> **B:** 8·92 24·57 13·06 35·75 18·3 5·649

Rub out some of the digits and ask your partner to work them out.

b Now choose one number from each list and come up with a subtracting calculation. Repeat three times and rub out some of the digits for your partner to work out.

Going deeper

1 a Using the key, can you work out the missing numbers in this calculation?

☆ = multiple of 4

▲ = multiple of 3

□ = multiple of 5

```
    ▲ □ 7 ▲
 +  □ ▲ □ ▲
 ─────────────
   ☆ ▲ ▲ □
```

b Can you write your own calculation for a partner using the same key?

Exploring percentages, fractions and decimals

Practice

1. Ravi's calculator is very simple, and doesn't have keys for fractions or percentages. Can you explain what calculations he can do to compare these two offers?

2. Decide which is greater in each of the pairs below. Can you explain how you know for each pair?

   a $\frac{2}{3}$ or 0·66   b 28% or $\frac{13}{50}$ c 0·75 or 80%

3. Which of the comparisons that you made in question 2 was easiest to decide? Can you explain why?

Going deeper

1. Esme sees a mountain bike in a shop sale. After a 30% discount, it would cost her £140. Then she sees a bike online that would cost her £160 after a 50% discount. Can you explain why the bike offered with the biggest discount actually costs more?

2. When or where have you noticed fractions being used outside school?

3. When or where have you noticed decimals being used outside school?

4. When or where have you noticed percentages being used outside school?

Comparing percentages

Three families' spend on food

	Murray	Wood	Novak
Vegetables	£2	£2	£5
Fruit	£4	£2	£6
Dairy	£11	£5	£8
Other	?	?	?
Total money spent	£20	£10	£20

Practice

1 a Look at how much money each family spent in total and how much they spent on fruit. Which family spent the highest percentage of their total money on fruit?

   b Which family spent the highest percentage of their total money on dairy?

   c Which family spent the lowest percentage of their total money on vegetables?

2 Which family spent the lowest percentage of their total money on other food?

3 Altogether, what percentage of their total money did these families spend on dairy?

Going deeper

1 Taken altogether, did these families spend more or less than 10% of their total money on vegetables? Can you explain how you know?

2 At Dylan's school during one week, Oak Class (35 children) had 7 absences, and Ash Class (30 children) had 3 absences.
Which class had the better attendance record for that week?
Can you explain why?

Percentage increases and decreases

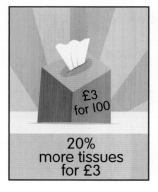

Practice

1 Which of the two offers above is better value? Can you explain why?

2 Choose a percentage increase from list B below, apply it to an amount from list A, and write down the increased amount. Can you do this for five different percentages and amounts in the lists?

> **A:** 22 km, 2 kg, 3820 ml, 7·8 ℓ, 840 cm², 6 miles, 358 seconds
>
> **B:** increases of: 1%, 5%, 7·5%, 10%, 15%, 70%, 95%

3 Choose a percentage discount from list D below, apply it to an amount from list C and then write down the reduced amount. Can you do this for five different percentages and amounts in the lists?

> **C:** £12, £48, £300, £245, £13·50, 80p
>
> **D:** discounts of: 5%, 7·5%, 25%, 33%, 60%, 62·5%

Going deeper

1 What is your best method for calculating 17·5% of £50? Can you explain your method to your partner?

2 If you add 20% on to an amount, and then take 10% off the total, will that give you the same result as taking 10% off the amount first and then adding 20% on? Can you explain why, or why not?

Using percentages with data

UK population at 2011 census ≈ 63 million

UK population by country at 2011 census

Country	Percentage of total population
England	84%
Northern Ireland	3%
Scotland	8%
Wales	5%

UK population by age at 2011 census

Age group	Percentage of total population
0–14 years	18%
15–64 years	66%
65 years and over	16%

Practice

1 a Roughly how many 0–14 year olds were living in the UK in 2011, do you think? Can you round your answer to the nearest 100 000?

   b Can you say roughly how many people lived in Wales in 2011?

   c Roughly how many people in the UK lived outside England in 2011?

2 In a bag of marbles, 20% are red. There are 15 red marbles. How many marbles are in the bag? Explain how you know.

Going deeper

1 Clara wants to increase this recipe by 25%. Can you work out what the new amounts will be for each ingredient, and how many rolls this new recipe will make?

Recipe for 8 sourdough rolls

240 g flour
30 g butter
50 ml water
30 g sugar
120 g sourdough starter
1 beaten egg (50 g)
1 pinch of salt

2 In the 30 years leading up to 2014, the number of sparrows in Europe fell by 147 million. This was a fall of roughly 60%. What do you think the number of sparrows in Europe was in 1984, to the nearest million? Can you explain your answer?

Exploring 2D shapes and angles

Tia is exploring all the different triangles she can make with a perimeter of 16 cm. She has found one so far.

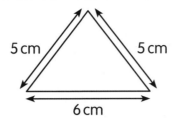

Practice

1 Draw Tia's triangle using a ruler and compass and then measure the angles with a protractor to the nearest degree. Can you label each angle and name the kind of triangle you have drawn?

2 Can you find any other triangles with a perimeter of 16 cm and sides that are a whole number of centimetres? Use a compass and ruler to draw, label and name each type of triangle.

3 Now can you draw some triangles with whole-number side lengths and a perimeter of 20 cm?

4 Using a ruler and a compass, can you construct a scalene triangle that is:

   a acute-angled   b obtuse-angled   c right-angled?

....

Going deeper

1 Look at your triangles from question 2. What generalizations can you make about the side lengths of a triangle with a perimeter of 16 cm? What side lengths can it not have? Explain why.

2 Two sides of a triangle are 8 cm and 5 cm, and the angle between these sides is 55°.

   a Can you draw the triangle using a compass, ruler and protractor? What is the other side length and the perimeter of the triangle?

   b What other triangles can you construct with the same perimeter (with whole-number side lengths)? Label the side lengths and angles. Can you make all 'types' of triangle? If not, why not?

   c Sort your triangles into categories.

Exploring quadrilaterals

Ryan is making
quadrilaterals and
using a branching
diagram to sort
them.

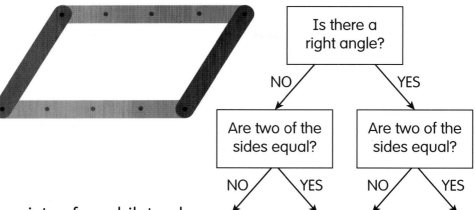

Practice

1 Draw or make a variety of quadrilaterals
using isometric paper or geo strips. Can you create four different
quadrilaterals that have two sets of equal sides?

 2 Can you create a branching diagram and use it to classify the
quadrilaterals you found in question 1?

Going deeper

1 Can you explore and explain if it is possible to create a quadrilateral
that has:

a three obtuse angles b three acute angles   c three right angles?

2 Which of these statements are sometimes true, always true or never
true? Can you explain your reasoning?

A square is a rhombus.

A trapezium is a rectangle.

A quadrilateral has two obtuse angles and two acute angles.

A parallelogram has one pair of obtuse angles.

Exploring angles in regular polygons

Shape	Number of sides or angles	Sum of interior angles	Size of each angle
Equilateral triangle	3	180°	60°
Square	4	360°	90°
Regular pentagon	5	540°	108°
Regular hexagon	6	720°	120°

Mindy has been exploring the sizes of interior angles in regular polygons.

Practice

 1 a Can you explain why the external angles of any polygon will always total 360°?

b Can you explain why the sum of the exterior and interior angles at any vertex make 180°?

2 What will the sum of the interior angles in an octagon be? Can you explain why?

 3 Can you work out what size the interior and exterior angles will be in a regular dodecagon (12-sided polygon)? Explain your reasoning to your partner.

Going deeper

1 Can you work out the sum of the internal angles in a regular heptagon?

2 Can you work out a formula for finding the size of the internal angles for any regular polygon with n sides?

heptagon

3 Investigate the number of triangles that can be drawn inside any polygon. Is there a generalization you can make?

Finding missing angles

I know angle ABC is 108° because the angles of a regular pentagon are 108°.

Practice

1 ABC forms an isosceles triangle, so can you calculate the other two angles in the triangle ABC? (angle BAC and angle BCA)

2 How could you calculate angle CAE?

3 Can you work out all the missing angles in the diagrams below?

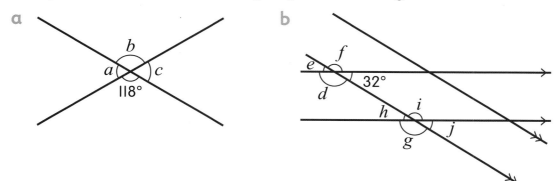

Going deeper

1 Can you draw the pentagon and five-pointed star above and then label the size of all the other angles? (Do not measure the angles with a protractor.)

2 Sketch a rhombus and show the diagonals within it. If one of the interior angles in the rhombus is 116°, can you label all the other angles within your drawing?

3 Create a missing angles problem for your partner, giving them the fewest number of angles they need to solve it.

Explorer Progress Book 6, pages 4–5

Exploring multi-step problems

Option A   Option B

£200

£150

£10

Practice

1 Owners of a new cafe want to be able to seat 40 customers. Can you help them decide which seating plan above is more cost effective? Can you explain the calculations you would use?

2 The owners estimate that up to 60 people will visit the cafe per hour and spend an average of £4·50 each. They want to find out how much money they could make in a day if they are open from 9 a.m. to 4 p.m.

   a Can you explain the steps you need to take to solve this problem?

   b Try to solve the problem using your steps. How can you check your answer?

Going deeper

1 Two adults and three children are going on a seven-day holiday. They think that every day each child will spend around €30 and each adult will spend around €75. They want to know how much they are likely to spend in total.

   a Can you list the steps they need to follow to work this out?

   b How can they check their calculations?

2 Sanjay buys 10 kg bags of salt to put on his driveway to melt snow. Each day he uses up 3 kg of salt. Salt costs 23p per kilogram. How much will he spend if the snow lasts a fortnight?

More multi-step problems

There are some posters on this classroom wall.

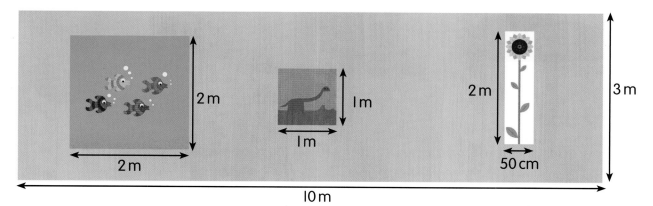

Practice

1 What percentage of this classroom wall is covered by posters?
Explain the steps you took to work this out.

 2 Using rulers or tape measures, can you find out the total areas of your classroom and the top of your desk? What units will you choose to work in?

 3 Work out approximately what percentage of your classroom floor would be visible when looking down directly from above. Can you explain how you arrived at your answer?

Going deeper

1 Each month, Aria saves 20% of her money, spends 30% of it on food, and spends the rest of it equally on music and clothes.
If she spends £120 more on food than music, how much money does Aria manage to save each month?

Can you draw a diagram to help you work this out?

2 In a park there are four times as many rabbits as squirrels. Birds make up the other 10% of the wildlife. If there are 40 birds, what percentage of the wildlife is squirrels, and how many are there?

BODMAS and the order of operations

Practice

1 Ron goes shopping and buys some of the items above. He works out his change using the calculation 2000 − 94 × 3 − 23 × 4.

Can you explain what Ron bought, how much he paid, and how much change he received?

2 Try to work out these calculations. Which one gives a different answer to the rest?

   a (3 × 10) − 2   b 3 × (10 − 2)   c 3 × 10 − 2   d (3 × 10 − 2)

 3 Now try these calculations. Which expressions have brackets that are unnecessary? Explain to a partner why the brackets are so important in the other expressions.

   a 1 + (2 × 3) + 4   b 1 + 2 × (4 − 3)   c 10 − 2 × 4
   d (10 − 2) × 4   e 10 − (2 × 4)

Going deeper

1 For a whole week you run 5 miles each morning and 3 miles each evening. Which of these calculations would you use to find the distance you run altogether? Can you explain how the brackets help?

   a 5 + 3 × 7   b 5 × 7 + 3 × 7   c (5 + 3) × 7   d 5 + (3 × 7)

2 Can you make up a word problem for each calculation below, so that the calculation gives the answer to that word problem?

   a 4 × £3·25 + £6·34   b 4 × (£3·25 + £6·34)
   c 20 kg − 1·5 kg × 4   d (20 kg − 1·5 kg) × 4

Using BODMAS to solve problems

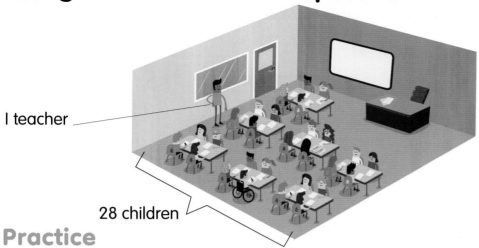

I teacher

28 children

Practice

1 There are 12 classes in a school. Each class has the same number of children and teachers as shown above. How many people are in the school altogether? Can you write a single calculation to show this, using brackets?

2 Can you work out these calculations?

a 14 ÷ 2 × 1 + 1

b 24 − (3 × 2 ÷ 3)

c $2^3 ÷ 2^4$

d 2 × 4 + 6 ÷ 8

e $3^2 ÷ 2 × 4 − 1$

f 72 ÷ (3 × 3) × 3

g $3^2 + 4^2 − 5^2$

h 4 × 3 − 2 ÷ 2 × 5

i 1 + 2 × 3 + 4 × 5

Going deeper

1 Can you copy these calculations and put, +, −, ×, or ÷ symbols in the boxes to make them correct? Add brackets where you need them.

a 4 ⬛ 2 ⬛ 6 = 16

b 4 ⬛ 2 ⬛ 6 = 12

c 4 ⬛ 2 ⬛ 6 = −4

d 4 ⬛ 2 ⬛ 6 = $\frac{1}{3}$

e 4 ⬛ 2 ⬛ 6 = 14

f 4 ⬛ 2 ⬛ 6 = 1

2 What possible answers can you find by putting any of +, −, ×, or ÷ symbols in the boxes below?

1 ⬛ 2 ⬛ 3 ⬛ 4 =

3 Repeat **question 2** but this time you are allowed to use exactly one pair of brackets. What new answers can you find?

Exploring ratio and proportion

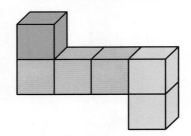

Practice

1 Look at the model above. Can you describe the ratios of the following colours in the model?

  a blue to yellow

  b green to blue

  c yellow to blue

2 Another model is made using 45 red and blue cubes in the ratio of 5 red to every 4 blue cubes.

  a How many red cubes will there be?

  b How many blue cubes will there be?

3 Can you find three different ways to illustrate each of these ratios?

  a 4:1   b 3:7   c 9:2   d 5:6

....

Going deeper

1 Tomo says that if you made a cube model that was twice as big as the one above, it would have four blue cubes. Do you think he is right? Can you explain your reasoning?

2 If Isobel made a larger model of the cube model above, that used 16 blue cubes, how many yellow cubes would it use? Can you write the ratio of yellow cubes to blue cubes, in this new model, in its simplest form?

Investigating ratio problems

Berry Delight

Recipe makes 3 glasses of juice.

Ingredients:
- 12 strawberries
- 18 blueberries
- 24 raspberries.

Practice

1 The recipe above will make three glasses of a mixed fruit juice. Can you work out how much fruit will be needed to make:

   a 5 glasses   b 12 glasses   c 7 glasses?

2 What proportion of the fruit is:

   a blueberries   b strawberries   c raspberries?

3 What do you think is the ratio of the following, in their simplest form:

   a blueberries to raspberries   b blueberries to strawberries

   c strawberries to raspberries?

Going deeper

1 Another juice recipe uses 84 berries in total from strawberries, blueberries, and raspberries in the ratios of 2:3:7 respectively. How many berries are used of each type? How can you check your answers?

2 If the ratios of the fruits in **question 1** had been 3:4:5 respectively, what fraction of the juice mixture would have been:

   a raspberries   b strawberries   c blueberries?

Examining ratio and proportion using pie charts

Owl Class healthy snack choices

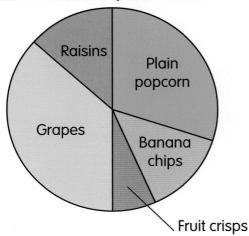

Healthy snack	Number of children
Fruit crisps	2
Grapes	11
Raisins	4
Plain popcorn	9
Banana chips	4

Practice

1 Owl Class surveyed their healthy snack preferences and recorded their results above. There are 420 children in the whole school, and the proportions of the whole school's favourite snacks are the same. Roughly how many children in the whole school prefer:

  a fruit crisps   b grapes   c raisins   d popcorn   e banana chips?

2 a What proportion of the children in Owl Class prefer grapes or popcorn?

  b What proportion of the children in Owl Class prefer fruit crisps or banana chips?

3 If the school bought 27 bags of popcorn for the children in the class, how many packets of grapes should they also buy?

4 If bags of popcorn are sold in boxes of 12 that cost £5·40 each, how much will enough packets for the whole school cost?

Going deeper

1 Of the 250 children in Dan's school, 36% were born in the autumn, 45 children were born in the winter, and $\frac{1}{5}$ of them were born in the spring. How many children do you think were born in the summer? How could you check your answer?

Unequal sharing problems

Practice

1 Look at the amount Annika's school raised for three charities. They agreed that for every £20 raised they would donate £4 to the wildlife sanctuary, £6 to their local hospital and £10 to the library. How much of the total money raised will go to each charity?

2 If they had raised £150, how much would have gone to each charity?

3 What percentage of their total money are they giving to:

a the wildlife sanctuary b the local hospital c the library?

School Raises £120

The supported charities are the wildlife sanctuary, the local hospital and the children's library.

Going deeper

1 Dario and Tom share some marbles between them in the ratio 4:6. When they finish sharing Tom has 16 more marbles than Dario. How many marbles did they share out?

 2 Can you make up a similar marble sharing problem for your partner to solve?

Exploring areas of 2D shapes

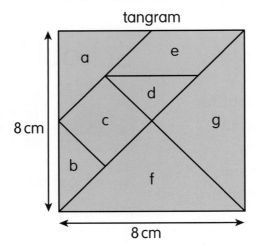

tangram

8 cm

8 cm

Practice

1 Nadeem draws a square that is 8 cm by 8 cm and then draws lines on it as shown above to make the seven pieces of a tangram. Can you work out the area of each of the seven pieces without measuring them? Explain how you did this.

2 If the area of Nadeem's square was 10 cm by 10 cm, and he cut it into the tangram shapes, what would the area of each piece be then?

Going deeper

1 Trace and cut out the tangram above.

a Can you use two pieces to create a quadrilateral that is exactly $\frac{5}{16}$ of the total area of the pieces? Can you explain your reasoning?

b Can you create a quadrilateral that is exactly $\frac{7}{16}$ of the total area of the pieces, again using just two of the pieces from the tangram? Can you explain your reasoning?

c Can you do the same thing but with three pieces?

2 Repeat **question** 1 but try to make pentagons that are $\frac{5}{16}$ and $\frac{7}{16}$ of the total area.

Finding the area of triangles

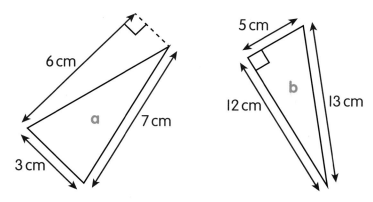

Practice

1 Can you find the areas of these triangles?

2 Can you explain why you think you are correct in each case?

Going deeper

Draw a 5 cm by 10 cm rectangle.
Label the corners A, B, C and D as
shown, then try this game.

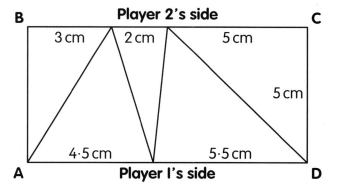

- Player 1 draws a straight line
  from point A up to anywhere
  on Player 2's side.

- Player 2 starts where the line
  ended, and draws a line back
  to Player 1's side.

- Keep taking turns to do this, until Player 1 draws a line to C or Player 2
  draws a line to D.

- The lines are not allowed to cross.

Calculate the area of all the triangles which have a base on your side.
Above, Player 1 has two triangles and Player 2 has three. The person
whose triangles add up to the largest total area is the winner.

  a Who won? Can you explain why?

  b Will this always happen? Why or why not?

Finding the area of parallelograms

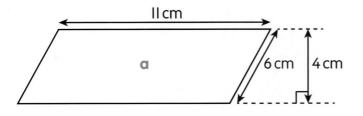

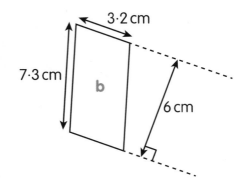

Practice

1 Can you calculate the areas of these two parallelograms?

2 Can you explain why you think you are correct?

Going deeper

1 What is the length of the base of this parallelogram?

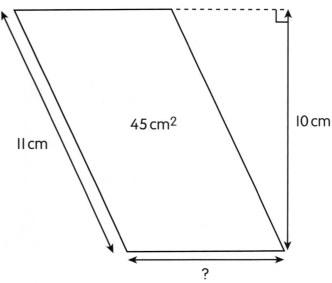

2 What is the value of the unknown number, x, in this parallelogram diagram?

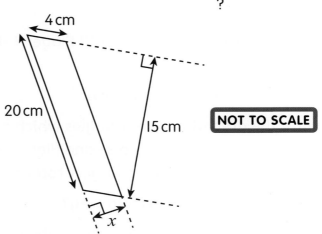

NOT TO SCALE

52

Problem solving with composite shapes

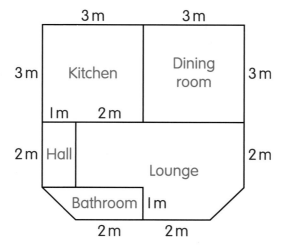

This is a plan of the ground floor of Omar's house.

Practice

1 a What is the area of each room?

   b The hall, lounge and bathroom are carpeted. Can you work out, what percentage of the total ground floor area is carpeted, to the nearest 5%?

Going deeper

1 a Can you draw a composite quadrilateral, made from a rectangle and a triangle, with an area of exactly 30 cm²?

   b Can you explain how you solved this problem?

2 a An isosceles trapezium is created by adding two triangles to a rectangle as shown below. If the total area of the shape is 50 cm², what are some possible dimensions of the shape?

   b How many possible answers could there be? Explain your reasoning.

Linking fractions with dividing

I have 3 apples. I want to share them equally between myself and my 3 friends.

Practice

1 How can Molly divide the apples equally? Can you write this as a dividing calculation to show what fraction of an apple they will each get?

2 How could Molly divide 3 apples equally between 6 people?

3 If the items below are shared equally, how much will each person get? Can you write each one as a dividing calculation? Express your answers in their simplest form.

    a 4 cheeses shared by 5 people   b 6 biscuits shared by 4 people

    c 8 sandwiches shared by 10 people   d 2 pies shared by 6 people

4 What is different about your answer to question 3b?

Going deeper

1 Can you find another way of sharing Molly's apples equally between her and her 3 friends that is different to your way in question 1?

2 Can you write your own sharing story for 3 ÷ 5 and then another for 5 ÷ 3 for a partner to solve?

3 Would you rather have 3 bars of chocolate shared between 4 people or 5 bars of chocolate shared between 6 people? Can you explain your thinking?

Making connections between fractions and decimals

Ben is writing all the fraction and decimal equivalents he knows. He is stuck on $\frac{1}{5}$.

$\frac{1}{2} = 0·5$ and $\frac{1}{4} = 0·25$
$\frac{1}{5} =$

Practice

1 a How many tenths are equivalent to $\frac{1}{5}$?

   b Can you draw a picture to show this?

2 What is $\frac{1}{5}$ as a decimal?

3 a Can you draw a **decimal** number line from 0 to 1 and mark on $\frac{1}{5}$, $\frac{2}{5}$, $\frac{3}{5}$, $\frac{4}{5}$, $\frac{5}{5}$ as decimals?

   b Now mark $\frac{1}{4}$ and $\frac{1}{2}$ as decimals on your number line.

4 If $\frac{1}{4} = 0·25$, what would $\frac{3}{4}$ be as a decimal?

Use your answer to **question 1** to help you.

Going deeper

1 If you know $\frac{2}{5}$ as a decimal, how can you work out $\frac{4}{5}$ as a decimal?

2 If 1 kg of modelling clay is shared equally by 8 children, can you work out how many grams of clay each child will get?

3 Write a decimal with one decimal place. Can your partner write the equivalent fraction in its simplest form? Take it in turns.

4 Write down any other fraction and decimal equivalents you know.

Fractions and recurring decimals

Parveen is exploring the patterns that some proper fractions make when she finds their decimal equivalents using a calculator.

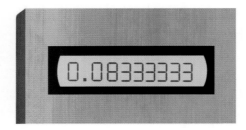

Practice

 1 One of the calculator displays above shows the decimal equivalent for $\frac{1}{11}$ and one shows the decimal equivalent for $\frac{1}{12}$. Can you say which is which? Discuss your reasoning with a partner.

2 Do you think that Parveen put the calculations into the calculator correctly? Check by using a written method to find the decimal equivalents for $\frac{1}{11}$ and $\frac{1}{12}$.

3 What do you think $\frac{2}{12}$ might be as a decimal?

4 Look at the fractions below. Can you estimate whether they will be greater than or less than 0·5 and explain why? Now work out the decimal equivalent for these fractions.

a $\frac{1}{3}$ b $\frac{5}{9}$ c $\frac{4}{7}$

Going deeper

1 Can you find a fraction that is a recurring decimal and is smaller than Parveen's?

2 Can you give a decimal that lies somewhere between $\frac{1}{4}$ and $\frac{1}{3}$?

 3 a Can you find a fraction that lies between 0·5 and 0·6 whose decimal equivalent is a recurring decimal? You can use a calculator. Discuss and explain your strategies for working this out.

b Repeat **question 3a** with a fraction that lies between 0·75 and 0·8.

Adding fractions and decimals

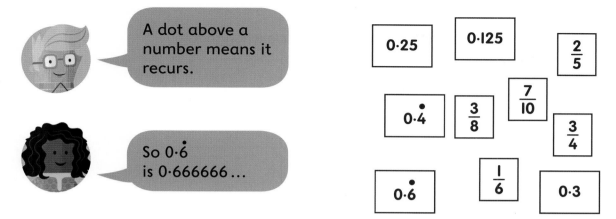

A dot above a number means it recurs.

So 0·6̇ is 0·666666...

Practice

 1 Can you put the numbers on the cards into the correct order from smallest to largest?

 2 Ben adds together $\frac{2}{5}$ and 0·25. Can you calculate what his answer should be? Discuss and explain the strategies you use.

3 Can you find the difference between $\frac{2}{5}$ and 0·25?

4 Look at the cards above. Can you find a pair of numbers that has a total of 1·05?

5 Can you work out the total and the difference for three other fraction and decimal pairs of cards?

Going deeper

1 Which fraction and decimal pairs above do you think are the simplest to add and find the differences between? Can you explain why you think so?

2 Can you find a pair that totals 0·466666...?

3 Which fraction and decimal pairs above will total more than 1? List them and then calculate the totals for each pair to check.

 4 Which fraction pairs do you think will have the smallest difference? Explore and try out your ideas by calculating the differences. Which fraction pairs have a difference less than 0·25?

Linear sequences and graphs

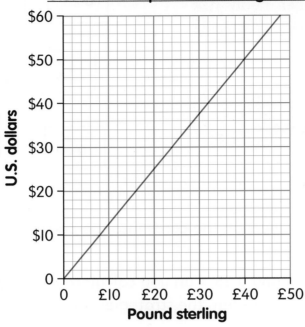

U.S. dollars to pounds exchange rate

Practice

1 Can you work out how many U.S. dollars you would be given for £40 using the graph above?

2 Can you use the information from the graph to draw a double number line, showing pound sterling values for $10, $20, $30, $40, and $50?

3 Can you explain what the general rule is for converting pounds to dollars in the graph above? How could you write this as a formula?

Going deeper

1 Can you write a formula for converting miles to kilometres? 1 mile is equivalent to 1·6 kilometres. Ask your partner to test your formula by calculating how far 3 miles is in kilometres.

2 Can you draw a graph that converts miles to kilometres, for a range of 0 to 50 miles?

3 From your graph, how far is 35 miles in kilometres?

4 Can you now write a formula for converting kilometres to miles?

Exploring number chains

Halve an even number. Add 5 to an odd number.

Practice

1 Try using Molly's rules to make number chains that begin with numbers 1 to 10. How many **different** number chains can you make? Explain the ways in which you think these number chains are different from each other.

2 What is the longest number chain that you can make like this, if you begin with the numbers 11 to 20 and stop when you reach a number that is repeated?

3 Now try exploring number chains made with these rules: halve an even number and add 5, and double an odd number. What do you notice?

Going deeper

1 Try using these number chain rules: halve an even number, and multiply an odd number by 4. What is the longest chain you can make beginning with the numbers 1 to 10, without repeating a number?

2 In **question 1** all the chains apart from the longest one repeat on the 4th move. Can you explain why this is?

3 Using the rules in **question 1**, but starting with numbers from 11 to 20, what do you notice? Which chains are the odd ones out, do you think? Can you explain why?

4 What do you think might happen with starting numbers up to 100?

Puzzles and generalizing

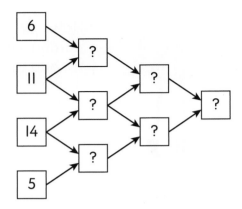

Practice

1 Can you predict what the final number will be in the number tree above, if numbers are added to produce the next level?

2 If the starting numbers are rearranged, can you predict which arrangements will produce the smallest final number?

3 Try exploring what happens if you write in the differences between numbers to get to the next level, rather than adding them. What do you notice?

Going deeper

1 If you write in the differences between numbers in a number tree, how can you arrange the starting numbers to produce the **highest** final number? Can you explain?

2 If you write in the differences between numbers in a number tree, how can you arrange the starting numbers to produce the **smallest** final number? Can you explain?

Growing sequences

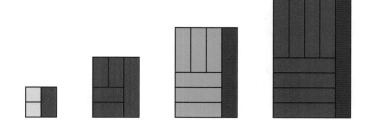

Practice

1 Can you draw, or make, the next step in this sequence with number rods? Can you describe the area of this new shape?

2 Now can you write a calculation for each term in the sequence?

3 Try to write a calculation for the 20th term in the sequence.

4 Can you write a calculation for the nth term in the sequence?

5 Can you each make a different, growing number rod pattern for your partner to describe? Write a calculation for the nth term of their sequence.

Going deeper

Sequence A: 9, 16, 23, 30, 37…
Sequence B: 1, 4, 9, 16, 25…

1 Try drawing two graphs of the two sequences above, putting the term numbers (i.e. positions in the sequence) along the horizontal axis, and the term values on the vertical axis.

2 What differences do you notice between the two graphs in **question 1**? Can you explain why one graph is straight and the other curves?

Exploring nets of cubes and cuboids

These two nets are the same, but one of them has been rotated.

Practice

1 Ben is exploring nets of cubes. Can you find as many as possible? Draw them on squared paper and compare your nets with your partner. Check that they are all different.

2 Can you explain what a polygon is? What about a polyhedron?

Going deeper

1 Can you explain why not all arrangements of six squares joined together are nets of cubes?

2 These six pieces of cardboard will make a box when put together.

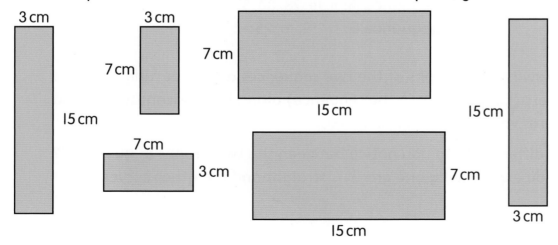

a Can you draw two nets and make the box from one of the nets?

b What is the volume of your box?

Investigating nets

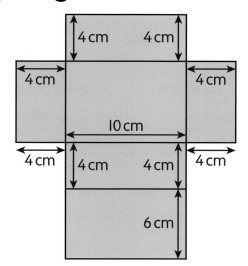

NOT TO SCALE

Practice

1 Will has bought Ava a watch for her birthday, and wants to make a gift box for it. Here is the net of a cuboid that Will thinks would be the ideal size.

  a Using a ruler, draw it accurately on squared paper or card.

  b Cut it out and assemble the gift box. Can you add tabs to help you fix the box together?

2 Can you work out the volume of the gift box? Can you explain how you know you have chosen the correct dimensions for your calculation?

....

Going deeper

1 A chocolate bar comes in a box shaped as a triangular prism. The box is 18 cm long and 5·2 cm tall. The ends are equilateral triangles with sides of 6 cm.

  a Can you draw a net for the box? Use a protractor and a ruler.

  b What other possible nets for this triangular prism can you find?

  c What is the total area of the net's five faces?

Platonic solids

The Greek mathematician Plato discovered that it is possible to make just five different 3D shapes in which:

Each face is the same regular polygon and the same number of faces meet at every vertex.

3D shape	Regular polygon used
Tetrahedron	Four equilateral triangles
Cube	Six squares
Octahedron	Eight equilateral triangles
Dodecahedron	Twelve regular pentagons
Icosahedron	Twenty equilateral triangles

tetrahedron

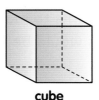

cube

octahedron

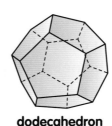

dodecahedron

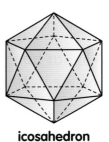

icosahedron

Practice

1 Can you draw both possible nets of a tetrahedron and then make the shape?

2 Can you draw a net of an octahedron and then make the shape?

Going deeper

1 Using a pentagon template, try to draw the net of a dodecahedron on a large sheet of paper. Cut it out and fold it up to check your work.

2 The 3D shapes which meet the rules Plato set are called the five 'Platonic solids'. Can you make a table showing how many faces, vertices and edges each one has?

Solving problems involving surface area and nets

Practice

1 A baker has created a cake called a tetra-sponge. It is in the shape of a regular tetrahedron and the net is shown here. She wants to cover each cake in edible foil.

12·1 cm

14 cm

a What is the total surface area of the piece of foil for each cake?

b If she is making a batch of 100 tetra-sponges, how many square metres of edible foil should she order?

Going deeper

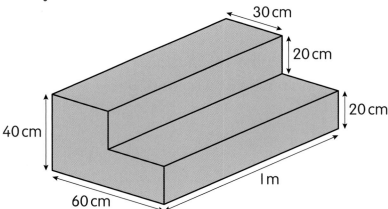

30 cm

20 cm

20 cm

40 cm

60 cm

1 m

1 Alice wants to make a fitted bag for her portable exercise steps shown here. Can you draw a net to help her work out how much fabric she will need?

2 Alice decides to dye the fabric. Bottles each contain enough dye to cover 2 m² of fabric. How many bottles of dye will she need to buy?

Multiplying using the short written method

Practice

 1 Discuss how you can estimate the answers here. After you have made your estimates, try copying and solving the calculations. How close were you?

a		3	0	7	5
	×				8

b	1	5	3	8	2
	×				6

2 By estimating, can you decide which calculations below will have an answer greater than 10 000? Copy and solve the calculations to find out if you were correct.

a	3	7	3	1
×				3

b	2	1	3	1
×				4

c	1	1	8	9
×				7

3 Natalia tries to solve this multiplying calculation. Is she correct? Can you explain why or why not by estimating?

	1	6	2	4
×				9
	9	5	1	6

Going deeper

1 Look at calculation in **question 1a** above. Can you think of a way to solve it mentally? Explain your method.

2 Eva estimates the answer to a multiplying calculation (ThHTO × O) to be 12 500. What could the calculation be? Can you find three possibilities which use a different multiplier each time?

Multiplying decimals

Practice

> I need six sheets of wrapping paper to wrap a present. Each sheet is 62·5 cm long.

1 Can you estimate the length of the paper if Molly joins all six sheets together? What will be the exact total length?

2 Can you copy and work out these calculations? Estimate first.

a	£ 4 · 2 8
	× 6

b	5 · 6 cm
	× 9

c	4 · 6 5 ℓ
	× 7

Going deeper

1 Molly from question 1 decides she needs three more sheets of paper. Discuss two different ways of working out the total length if she combines all the sheets together.

2 What would you do if you had to multiply the amounts below using a calculator with a broken decimal point key? Estimate first, then solve the calculations without using the decimal points.

a	£ 6 · 8 2
	× 8

b	3 4 · 8 km
	× 6

c	5 2 · 7 m
	× 4

3 Which of these calculations are incorrect? How do you know? What might have gone wrong?

> 18·8 cm × 9 = 169·2 mm
> 43·3 km × 5 = 216 500 m
> 32·6 ℓ × 7 = 2282 ℓ

Using long multiplication: whole numbers and decimals

A school library has £1000 to spend on new books and places this order.

Book type	Price	Quantity
Picture books	£3·65	15
Fantasy	£7·50	18
Fairy tales	£5·25	14
Non-fiction	£9·98	24
Poetry	£6·75	28
Box sets	£18·00	16

Practice

I Using long multiplication, can you work out:

a how much the school spends on each book type

b how much the school spends in total?

Going deeper

I This is Jacob's strategy for working out the cost of the picture books. Can you explain it and how it relates to long multiplication?

Jacob

×	3	0·6	0·05
10	30	6	0·5
5	15	3	0·25

2 Repeat **question** I using Sita's strategy, shown here. What does she need to do to her answer?

Sita

×	300	60	5
10	3000	600	50
5	1500	300	25

3 Using the digits 4–9, can you create a calculation that will give you a product less than 400 000?

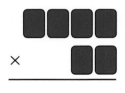

Problem solving using long multiplication

Olivia has set up a key for her puzzles. Each symbol represents a whole single digit.

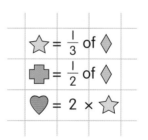

Practice

1 Can you work out what each symbol is worth and find the answers to these calculations?

2 Can you make up some of your own puzzles using these symbols for your partner to solve?

Going deeper

1 Olivia introduces a new symbol to her key (⚡): Can you work out what this symbol must be worth?

2 Can you create your own key and then give your partner a multiplying calculation to solve? Make sure it is possible to solve!

3 Can you find a multiplying calculation that will give a product between 65 000 and 75 000?

Using long dividing to solve sharing problems

We have 512 books to share equally between 16 classes.

Practice

 1 a Can you explain how to use the long written method of dividing to share the books equally? Use the words below.

hundreds	exchange	share	tens	ones

b Can you use the inverse to check the answer?

2 There are 1296 bottles of orange squash and 18 crates. Can you work out how many bottles are in each crate?

Going deeper

1 Can you write a sharing word problem for the calculations below, and then solve them?

a 216 ÷ 12　　　　**b** 780 ÷ 15　　　　**c** 1508 ÷ 26

2 Can you choose one number from each box to make three different dividing sentences that are correct? Do some estimating first.

315	1476	888

12	18	21

82	15	74

Using long dividing to solve grouping problems

Popcorn tubs come in boxes of 35 and a cinema needs 945 tubs.

```
            2  7
  3  5 ) 9  4  5
         7  0  0   (20 × 35)
         2  4  5
         1  7  5   (5 × 35)
            7  0
            7  0   (2 × 35)
               0
```

I've worked out how many boxes to order.

Practice

1 a Can you explain Molly's method for solving the problem above?

   b Can you use the inverse to check Molly's answer?

   c If the cinema needs 1500 tubs, how many boxes should it order?

2 On a trip, every group of 12 children must go with 1 adult. How many adults are needed if there are 200 children?

3 Theatre tickets cost £56 and a drama club has £1800. How many tickets can they buy?

Going deeper

1 Dan is checking some of Anita's dividing calculations by multiplying. Can you work out what the dividing calculations must have been?

   a 22 × 126 + 13   b 12 × 254 + 8

2 Which calculations below do you think will leave a remainder? Can you explain your reasoning and then solve each calculation?

   a 3572 ÷ 25   b 1236 ÷ 12   c 2740 ÷ 19   d 928 ÷ 16

Solving dividing problems with remainders

We have raised £678 and want to share this between 12 different charities.

We have raised £852 and want to share this between 16 different charities.

Ben   Tia

Molly   Ravi

Practice

1 How much will each charity receive from Ben and Tia? Can you explain how to divide the remaining whole pounds between their 12 charities?

2 Can you estimate how much Molly and Ravi's charities will each receive and then work out the exact amounts?

3 Can you solve 1302 cm ÷ 24? Try estimating first. How close were you?

4 Can you solve 2455 ml ÷ 25? Try estimating first. How close were you?

Going deeper

1 Ben and Tia raise a further £69. How much will each of their 12 charities receive now? Can you explain your thinking to a partner?

2 Molly and Ravi raise a further £300. How much extra will each of the 16 charities receive?

3 Look at these partial calculations. Can you work out the missing amounts (dividends) for each? Explain to a partner how you solve these.

```
        2 1·5 cm                    1 8 0·2 5 ml
  3 6 )▢ ▢ ▢              2 8 )▢ ▢ ▢ ▢
```

Dividing decimals equally using long or short dividing

A different number of people sat at each table below and shared their bill equally. The bills divided exactly.

Table 1

Bill
£45·72

Table 2

Bill
£95·80

Table 3

Bill
£165·75

12 people

15 people

20 people

Practice

 1 a Match the number of people who were sitting at each table with the correct bill. Can you explain your thinking and your calculations?

   b For each bill amount, can you find three other divisors that you could divide the amount by, resulting in equal shares?

2 If a piece of rope is 3·85 m long and is divided into 14 equal pieces, can you work out how long each piece will be in centimetres?

Going deeper

 1 Can you write three other table bill totals that will divide between a number of people to give exactly equal shares?

2 a Can you find five different divisors that will divide £24·80 exactly?

   b Can you find three different divisors that will divide £146·25 exactly?

3 How many different ways can you divide 5·6 m of string exactly into equal pieces of at least 20 cm? Use whole numbers of centimetres. Can you say how long each piece will be?

Exploring volume and scaling

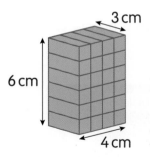

Practice

1 a Can you work out the volume of this cuboid?

   b Can you sketch it in another orientation?

   c How many other cuboids can be made with the same volume, if all the edges have to be a whole number of centimetres? How do you know that you are correct?

2 Can you describe all possible cuboids with a volume of 40 cm³, with side lengths that are whole numbers of centimetres? How do you know that you are correct?

Going deeper

1 Can you work out the volume of this triangular prism?

2 Another triangular prism has a volume of 60 cm³, and sides with whole numbers of centimetres. What possible dimensions could it have? Can you draw three different examples?

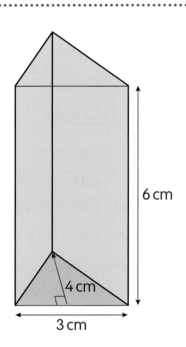

Solving volume problems

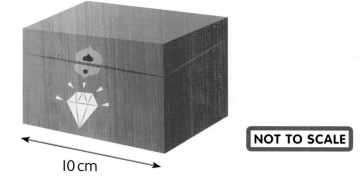

Volume: 480 cm³

10 cm

NOT TO SCALE

Practice

1 Laura's jewellery box has a volume of 480 cm³. It is 10 cm long. What might the other two dimensions be? Can you explain your thinking?

2 A designer is trying to create a gift box in the shape of a cube. Its sides all need to be whole numbers of centimetres, and the box needs to have a volume of at least 200 cm³. What is the smallest box she could design?

Going deeper

1 A large building block has a volume of 1500 cm³. If it has a square cross-section, and is 1·5 times as long as it is wide, can you find its dimensions?

2 Aysha has 100 dice to post to a school. Each dice measures 2 cm in each direction. Before posting, Aysha wraps up the dice in a cuboid-shaped parcel. Aysha knows that the school's letterbox is 5 cm high by 20 cm long.

What dimensions would you suggest for the parcel? Can you explain your reasoning to a partner and explain how you worked this out?

Units of volume

Capacity:
500 000 ml
or
500 000 cm³

Practice

I For each of the following, write down whether you think they would be better measured in mm³, cm³, m³, or km³:

a milk for a cake recipe

b medicine for a cough

c annual rainfall for a town

d air on a submarine

e concrete for a patio

f a slice of apple pie.

2 Printer ink costs about £3 per cm³. How much would 1ℓ of printer ink cost?

3 How much would 1m³ of printer ink cost?

Going deeper

I Two beach volleyball courts are being built, each measuring 5 m by 9 m, and they need sand to a depth of 50 cm all over.

a How much sand is needed?

b A builder delivers sand at a cost of £25 per m³. How much will the builder charge?

c A windstorm blows all the sand away from one of the courts. Can you work out how much sand would need to be re-ordered?

2 Sand used to be sold in cubic yards instead of cubic metres. Discuss with a partner what you would need to know in order to work how many cubic yards of sand would be needed for the two courts.

Scaling and scale factors

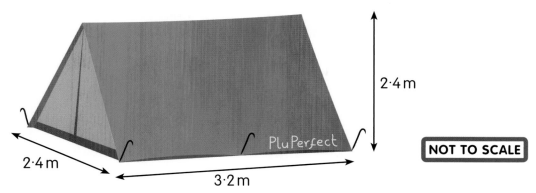

2·4 m

2·4 m

3·2 m

PluPerfect

NOT TO SCALE

Practice

I Paul is a tentmaker. The dimensions of Paul's favourite tents, the PluPerfect range, are shown above.

a What is the volume of a PluPerfect tent?

b Paul wants to make a model of his tent that is smaller by a scale factor of 8. What will the new dimensions be?

c What would be the volume of the model? Is this the result that you expected? Can you explain your reasoning?

Going deeper

I An architect is designing an office building and wants to show his client a scale model of how the finished building will look. The actual building is going to be a cuboid 10 m high, with a base of 20 m by 20 m. It will have an inner square courtyard of 5 m by 5 m.

a Find the area of the base of the building in m^2.

b Find the volume of the building in m^3.

c If the model is 1 m high, find the dimensions of the base of the model.

d What is the area of the base of the model? Can you write it in cm^2 and m^2?

e What is the volume of the model?

 Explorer Progress Book 6, pages 10–11

Adding and subtracting with fractions

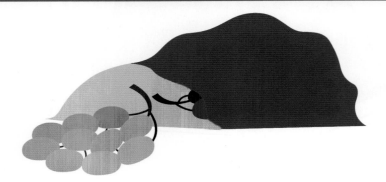

Practice

1 a Ed buys a bag of mixed grapes. He notices that $\frac{3}{5}$ of them are red and the rest are green. Can you write what fraction is green?

   b Ed counts the green grapes. There are 10. How many grapes are in the bag altogether? Can you explain how you worked it out?

   c Ed eats $\frac{1}{5}$ of the grapes for breakfast and $\frac{2}{5}$ of the grapes at lunchtime. What fraction of the grapes are left?

2 a If $\frac{3}{9}$ of a red, white and blue flag is painted blue, and $\frac{2}{9}$ is painted white, what fraction is painted red?

   b Can you design a flag which uses these colours and proportions?

Going deeper

1 Three children took part in a sponsored run. Kamal raised three times as much money as Britney, and Theo raised five eighths of the total money.

   a If Britney raised £7·50, how much did Kamal and Theo each raise?

   b How much did they raise in total?

2 Sammi's secret sauce is $\frac{1}{7}$ tomato purée, $\frac{2}{7}$ milk and the rest is water. Sammi needs to make 3·5 litres of sauce. Can you work out how much of each ingredient she will use?

Adding and subtracting fractions whose denominators are multiples of the same number

Practice

1 If Ben takes $\frac{2}{5}$ of the cake and Tia takes $\frac{3}{10}$ of the cake, how much of the cake is left? Can you explain?

2 Alicia spends $\frac{1}{6}$ of her pocket money on a bus ticket and $\frac{1}{2}$ of it on a cinema ticket. Can you write what fraction of the money she has left?

3 Can you work out how much bigger $\frac{4}{5}$ is than $\frac{1}{10}$?

4 Can you work out the difference between $\frac{1}{3}$ and $\frac{5}{6}$?

··

Going deeper

1 Can you estimate which is the largest and the smallest fraction in this list? Write them out in **ascending** order to check.

$$\frac{2}{3} \qquad \frac{13}{18} \qquad \frac{5}{6} \qquad \frac{7}{9}$$

2 Rob wrote these equations, but he smudged some of the numbers.

a How many pairs of missing numbers can you find to make this equation balance?

b Assuming these equations were correct, what might the missing numbers have been?

$$\frac{\boxed{}}{\boxed{5}} + \frac{\boxed{}}{\boxed{10}} = \frac{\boxed{18}}{\boxed{20}}$$

$$\frac{\boxed{3}}{\boxed{}} + \frac{\boxed{}}{\boxed{5}} = \frac{\boxed{13}}{\boxed{15}}$$

Adding and subtracting more fractions

$\frac{1}{3}$ off the original price for all loyalty card holders

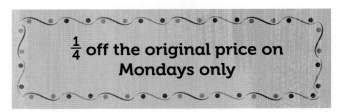

$\frac{1}{4}$ off the original price on Mondays only

Practice

1 Can you work out what overall discount loyalty card holders would get on Mondays (assuming they are entitled to both discounts)?

2 If $\frac{1}{3}$ of the class has brown hair and $\frac{1}{5}$ has blonde hair, what fraction of the class has hair that is neither blonde nor brown?

3 Three sisters share a pie. Emily gets $\frac{1}{4}$, Martina gets $\frac{2}{5}$ and Selina gets the rest. Can you work out what fraction of the pie Selina gets?

Going deeper

1 Francia is training for a triathlon – she must swim, cycle and run. Francia estimates that she will spend $\frac{7}{12}$ of her time running and $\frac{1}{8}$ of her time swimming. What fraction of her time does Francia expect to spend cycling?

2 Matt the builder is fetching bricks from his truck. He fetches $\frac{1}{4}$ of the bricks at 8 a.m., another $\frac{1}{4}$ at 9 a.m., and another $\frac{1}{4}$ at 10 a.m. By 11 a.m. Matt realizes he has more than enough bricks, so he returns the unused ones to his truck. He notices that the truck now contains $\frac{1}{3}$ of the bricks he had originally. Can you work out what fraction of the bricks Matt put back?

Using arrays to support calculating with fractions

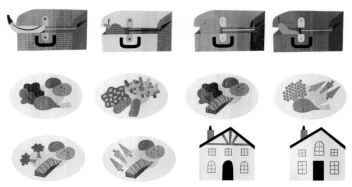

Practice

1 **a** In school, $\frac{1}{3}$ of the children bring a packed lunch and $\frac{1}{2}$ have a school dinner. Using the image at the top of the page, can you explain what fraction of the children this is altogether?

b The rest of the children go home for lunch. Can you work out what fraction of children this is?

2 $\frac{2}{5}$ of the class say tennis is their favourite sport while $\frac{1}{4}$ say that football is their favourite. What fraction of the class voted for a different sport? Explain your answer by drawing an array.

3 Asma's cat spends $\frac{1}{3}$ of his day asleep and $\frac{1}{4}$ of his day out in the garden. Can you work out what proportion of his day that is altogether?

Going deeper

1 How can you show that $\frac{2}{3} + \frac{3}{4}$ is equal to $1 + \frac{5}{12}$ using or drawing an array? Do you need more than one array?

2 Jake has added two fractions together, and has drawn this array to check his answer. What might the calculation have been? Can you find all the possibilities?

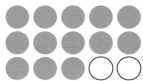

Understanding multiplying fractions

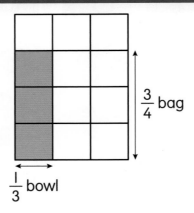

$\frac{3}{4}$ bag

$\frac{1}{3}$ bowl

Practice

1 Freya pours $\frac{3}{4}$ of a bag of nuts into a bowl. She then eats $\frac{1}{3}$ of the nuts in the bowl. Can you use this diagram to explain what fraction of the bag has been eaten?

2 Austin also has a bag of nuts. He too pours $\frac{3}{4}$ into a bowl, but then eats $\frac{2}{3}$ of the nuts in the bowl. Can you draw a diagram similar to the one used in question 1 and explain how you would use it to find out what fraction of Austin's bag has been eaten?

Going deeper

1 Take it in turns to make up a fraction question to go with the diagrams below. Ask your partner to solve the question and explain their reasoning, then check their answer.

a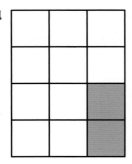

b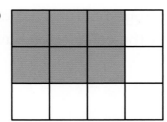

c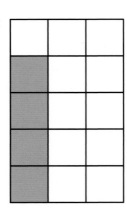

Multiplying two fractions using a fraction machine

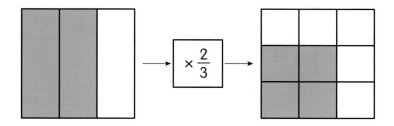

Practice

1 Can you explain what calculation the above fraction machine is doing, and find the answer?

2 Can you draw a fraction machine to show how to calculate:

   a $\frac{3}{4} \times \frac{1}{2}$ b $\frac{5}{7} \times \frac{1}{3}$ c $\frac{3}{5} \times \frac{1}{4}$ d $\frac{3}{4} \times \frac{1}{4}$

   e the product of $\frac{1}{2}$ and $\frac{3}{4}$?

3 What do you notice about your results? Talk to a partner about your findings.

Going deeper

1 Mrs Pennington is teaching her class how to make a fraction machine out of Numicon Shapes to multiply fractions together. Below are pictures of the two things she shows them. Can you work out what two fractions Mrs Pennington might be multiplying together, and explain how to find the answer?

2 Can you now use Numicon Shapes to make up and illustrate your own question for your partner to answer?

Multiplying two fractions using a general rule

Practice

1 $\frac{3}{4}$ of a salad is covered with tomatoes, and then $\frac{2}{3}$ of that section is topped with mayonnaise. What fraction of the original salad contains both tomatoes and mayonnaise? Can you illustrate the problem to check your answer?

2 A packet of biscuits claims to have $\frac{1}{2}$ of my 'recommended daily allowance (RDA) of sugar'. If I were to eat $\frac{1}{3}$ of the biscuits, what fraction of my RDA of sugar would I have had?

3 $\frac{2}{3}$ of a class go to the park and $\frac{3}{4}$ of those play football. What fraction of the class is now playing football? Can you explain the general rule you used to find the answer?

Going deeper

1 George gives $\frac{2}{3}$ of a cake to his daughter. She gives $\frac{2}{3}$ of what she receives to her friends. What fraction of George's original cake do the friends have? What fraction of George's original cake does his daughter have at the end?

2 Sara types $\frac{3}{4}$ into her calculator and then gives it to Luke. He presses '×', types another fraction, then presses '='. The calculator now displays $\frac{1}{2}$. Without using a calculator, can you find out some possible fractions that Luke might have typed in?

3 Which pairs of cards would you need to multiply together to make each of these fractions?

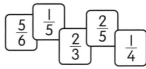

a $\frac{1}{3}$ b $\frac{4}{15}$ c $\frac{1}{10}$ d $\frac{1}{6}$

Dividing a proper fraction by a whole number

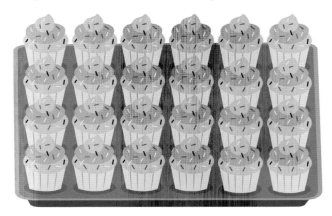

Practice

1 Ali has baked this tray of 24 cupcakes. He tells his two children they may eat one third of the cupcakes between them.

   a Assuming they share equally, what fraction of the cakes will each child eat?

   b How many cakes does that represent? Can you draw an array to illustrate the problem and explain how to use it to check your answer?

2 Try to find the value of:

   a $\frac{3}{5} \div 3$ b $\frac{3}{5} \div 4$ c $\frac{3}{5} \div 5$

Going deeper

1 a A tub of ice cream is $\frac{3}{5}$ full. If 3 children share the ice cream equally, what fraction of the ice cream would each child get?

   b If the tub contained $\frac{1}{2}\ell$ of ice cream when full, how much ice cream did each child eat?

2 Saskia spends $\frac{1}{3}$ of her pocket money and saves the rest. She spends the same amount on comic books, fruit, stationery and toys. What fraction of her pocket money does she spend on each of these items?

Solving empty box problems

$$\blacksquare + 34 = 60$$

$$\blacksquare + \blacksquare = 60$$

$$\blacksquare + 34 = \blacksquare$$

Practice

1 If the answers to the empty box problems above are all positive whole numbers, how many possible answers will there be to each problem? Can you explain why?

2 Using the prime factors of 462, can you find three different solutions to the empty box problem below?

$$\blacksquare \times \blacksquare \times \blacksquare = 462$$

3 Can you find two different solutions to each of the following empty box problems and explain them to your partner?

$$\blacksquare \div \blacksquare = 20 \qquad \blacksquare \div \blacksquare \div \blacksquare = 20$$

Going deeper

1 Can you explain how to solve this unknown number problem, using the number trio?

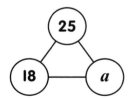

2 Can you write four different number sentences involving the letter a, based on this **multiplying** number trio?

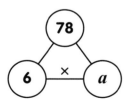

3 How many different solutions can you find to this empty box problem?

$$\frac{\blacksquare}{\blacksquare} \times \frac{\blacksquare}{\blacksquare} = \frac{15}{22}$$

Symbolic notation

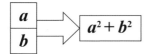 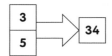

Practice

1 Can you work out the rule for this diagram, and write it using the letters a and b?

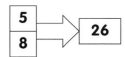

2 Look at the diagram below. Can you write three different input pairs (a, b) that give outputs in the range 60–90?

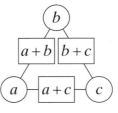

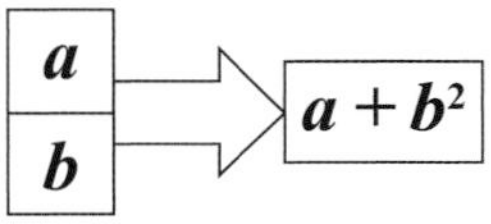

3 Can you rewrite these more simply?

   a $a + b + b + c$ b $b + c + c + d$

4 Can you add your answers to question 3a and 3b together into one expression?

....

Going deeper

1 In the diagram on the right, if you compare the total of the numbers in the rectangles with the total of the numbers in the circles, what do you notice? Can you explain?

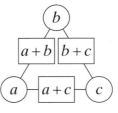

2 Can you work out the rule for this diagram, and write it using the letters a, b and c? Can you find more than one possibility?

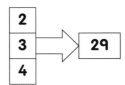

Solving problems with algebra

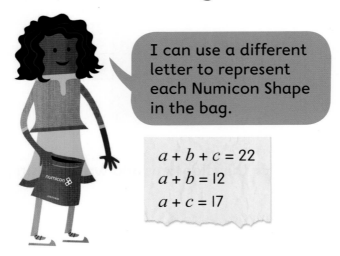

I can use a different letter to represent each Numicon Shape in the bag.

$$a + b + c = 22$$
$$a + b = 12$$
$$a + c = 17$$

Practice

 1 Can you use Numicon Shapes to help you work out which ones Tia has in her bag? Explain your reasoning to your partner.

2 Can you work out the values of the coloured counters in the boxes below?

a 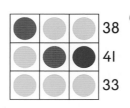 24 18 37   b 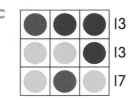 38 41 33   c 13 13 17   d 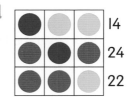 14 24 22

Going deeper

1 Can you work out the values of a, b, and c below? Using the letters a, b, and c, can you explain how you worked this out?

a	b	b	10
c	a	a	10
b	c	b	14

2 If $a \times b \times c = 126$, $a \times b = 18$, and $b \times c = 63$, can you work out the values of a, b and c? Explain your reasoning to your partner.

Finding all possibilities

The vehicles in this car park have 36 wheels in total.

Practice

1 Using number rods, can you suggest how many bicycles and how many cars might be in the car park? How many different possibilities can you find?

2 If there were 15 vehicles altogether, how many of these were cars and how many were bicycles do you think? Can you explain?

3 Can you write down the relationship between the numbers of bicycles and cars, and the number of wheels? Use W to stand for the number of wheels, a to stand for the number of bicycles and b to stand for the number of cars.

Going deeper

1 If the car park attendant counted a total of 52 wheels and 21 vehicles (cars and bicycles) altogether, how many do you think were cars, and how many were bicycles?

2 Can you explain your strategy for working out the answer to **question 1**? Do you have to calculate 'wheel totals' for every possible pair of numbers from (1, 20) through to (20, 1), or can you rule out some possible pairs without needing to find a total?

Exploring circles

Amy is looking at an orange slice and can see different parts of a circle on it.

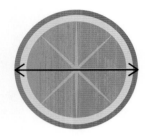

Practice

1 Amy measures the longest distance across the orange slice. What do we call this part of a circle?

2 a If this length is 8 cm, can you estimate the circumference of the orange slice? Explain how you came up with this estimate.

   b Can you use a compass to draw a circle with a diameter of 8 cm and measure the circumference to see how close your estimate was?

3 The radius, diameter and circumference are not all shown on the fruit slices below. Can you work out the missing measurements? Round your answers to 2 decimal places.

a

4·8 cm

b

33 cm

c

NOT TO SCALE

4·5 cm

Going deeper

1 Can you write a formula that shows how Amy could work out the circumference of the cross-section of the orange?

2 Using a compass, draw three different circles on a piece of paper. Label one part of the circle with the correct measurement, and ask your partner to calculate the other dimensions so that the radius, diameter and circumference are labelled.

Using the relationship between diameter and circumference

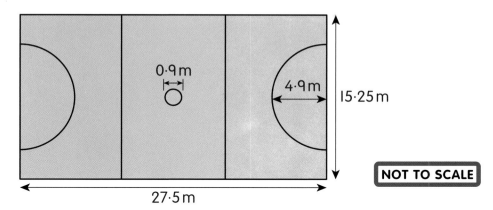

0·9 m

4·9 m

15·25 m

NOT TO SCALE

27·5 m

Zara's school has marked up a new netball court.

Practice

1 The circumference of a circle is about 3·14 times the length of its diameter. Can you work out the circumference of the centre circle?

2 Can you work out the circumference of the **semicircle** used for scoring goals? Can you explain to a partner how you chose to work this out?

3 Can you work out the circumference of a circle with a **radius** of:

   a 2·3 feet   b 1·5 km   c 5 mm?

··

Going deeper

1 Can you draw the netball court above using a scale of 1 m = 1 cm?

2 Using the formula $C \approx 3\cdot14d$, can you work out what the diameters of the circles below must be, to 2 decimal places? You may use a calculator.

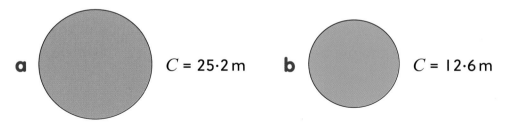

a $C = 25\cdot2$ m   b $C = 12\cdot6$ m

91

Solving circle problems

Speed sign

The red rim of this speed sign is 3 cm wide.

The diameter of this speed sign is 22·5 cm.

Practice

1 Can you calculate the circumference of the speed sign to 2 decimal places?

2 Can you calculate the circumference of the white circle on the speed sign to 2 decimal places?

3 a Can you recreate this pattern? The space between each circle is 1 cm and the radius of the smallest green circle is 1·5 cm.

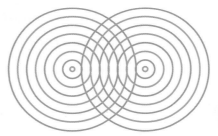

NOT TO SCALE

b What is the circumference of the biggest purple circle?

Going deeper

1 A slice is cut out of a circular pie. It is cut from the centre and each straight edge of the slice is 9 cm long. Can you work out the overall circumference of the pie? Explain how you solved this.

2 Can you estimate the length of a slice of pie if the circumference of the pie is approximately 30 cm? Will the pie be bigger or smaller than that above?

Solving more problems

Practice

 1 If a circle doubles its diameter, does it double its circumference too?
Explore to work out if this is true or not.

2 a Can you work out the circumference of gear A below?

   b Can you work out the diameter and circumference of gear B?

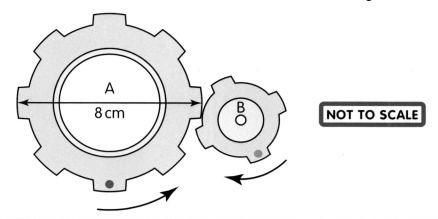

NOT TO SCALE

> Gear A has a diameter of 8 cm and gear B's diameter is half as long. Gear
> B completes two whole rotations for every one whole rotation of gear A.
>
> When the red dot returns to its starting point, gear A has completed one
> whole rotation and the dot has travelled the length of the circumference
> of gear A. Likewise, when the blue dot returns to its starting point, it has
> travelled the length of the circumference of gear B.

Going deeper

 1 If Dalbir turns gear A two complete rotations, how far will the blue dot
on gear B travel in centimetres? Explain your reasoning to a partner.

2 How far (in centimetres) will the red dot on gear A travel if gear B
turns $2\frac{1}{2}$ rotations?

3 If gear A turns 12 rotations, how far (in centimetres) will the blue dot
on gear B travel?

Solving non-routine problems using all four operations

The PE teacher times the swimming team as the children swim lengths of the pool. Here are their results.

	Name	Number of lengths	Time (minutes)
1	Anita	10	3
2	Isaac	12	4
3	Shona	8	2
4	Alistair	15	3

Practice

1 a Estimate who swam the fastest and who swam the slowest. What did you do to decide? Which calculations were you able to do mentally?

 b Share your methods with a partner. Did you do them in the same way?

 2 Can you predict how far each swimmer can swim in 10 minutes, if they swim at a constant speed? Explain your reasoning to your partner.

Going deeper

1 The four swimmers have a race to swim four lengths of the pool.
If each swimmer swims at a constant speed, by how many seconds will the winner beat the second-place swimmer?

Can you explain how you worked out the answer?

Solving non-routine problems using fractions and percentages

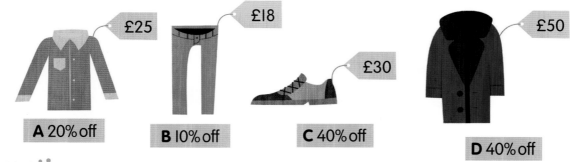

A 20% off   B 10% off   C 40% off   D 40% off

Practice

1 Which of these discounts would save you the most money?

2 Joel buys all four items above. How much change does he save, compared to buying all four items at full price?

3 The shopkeeper buys the items for half of their original selling price. How much profit will they make on each item if they sell at the sale price?

Going deeper

1 There are five pairs of socks for Emilia to choose from. She buys three pairs and spends exactly £10·57. Which three pairs did she buy?

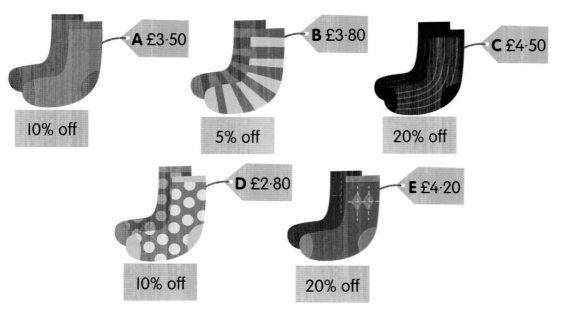

Solving non-routine problems – multiplying and dividing

Mo

Rachel

55 cm

45 cm

Practice

1 If Rachel and Mo both cycle the same distance, whose wheels will have to turn more times? Can you explain?

2 Can you estimate how far Rachel and Mo would each travel if their wheels completed 10 complete rotations?

3 Rachel and Mo both cycle in a straight line until their wheels have turned through 100 rotations. Can you say who is further ahead, and by how much?

Going deeper

1 Both Rachel and Mo cycle for exactly 1 km. Approximately how many complete revolutions do:

a Rachel's wheels turn through

b Mo's wheels turn through?

2 My racing bike has a revolution counter. I notice that after cycling 210 m it says that the wheels have turned 70 revolutions. Can you work out the approximate diameter of my wheels?

Further non-routine problems

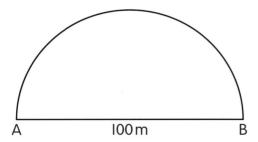

A   100m   B

Practice

1 Rajesh runs at 10 metres per second and walks at 2·5 metres per second. He runs the 100m from A to B in a straight line, and then walks back to A around the semicircle. Can you work out how much further he walks than runs?

2 If Rajesh runs the entire distance, instead of walking part of it, how much sooner do you think he will he get back to point A?

3 If he walks the entire route, can you work out how much longer it takes him than if he runs the whole route?

Going deeper

1 Approximately how many times longer is the semicircle than the straight path? What did you do to answer this?

2 Leo is also training. He runs around the semicircle from B to A, and then walks back to B along the straight path, while Rajesh runs the straight section and walks the curve. If Leo and Rajesh both run and walk at the same speeds as each other, can you work out who will finish first?

Exploring the four quadrants

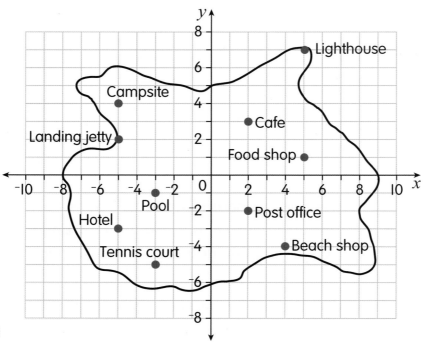

Practice

1 Can you give the coordinates of the landmarks in each quadrant?

2 At what points does the edge of the island cross the axes?

Going deeper

👥 1 Can you draw your own island on a coordinate grid with these landmarks in the correct places? Can you predict what quadrant each will appear in, and explain why you think this?

Caravan site (6,2)
Restaurant (-3·5,4)
Park (-5,-5·25)
Tea shop $(2\frac{3}{4}, -8)$
Reception (0,0)

👥 2 Without your partner seeing, draw a picture on a four quadrant coordinate grid using only straight lines. Give your partner instructions to re-create your picture. Can you use all these words at least once?

x-axis   y-axis   origin   quadrant   coordinate
positive   negative   point

Translation in four quadrants

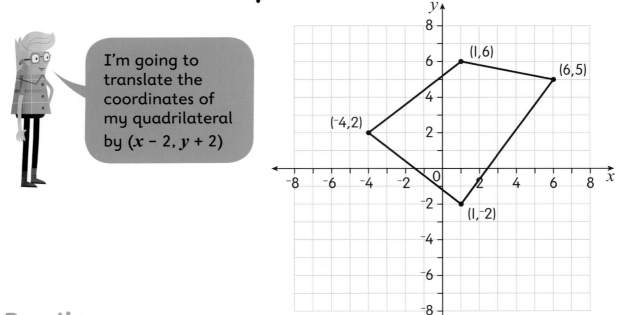

I'm going to translate the coordinates of my quadrilateral by $(x - 2, y + 2)$

Practice

1 Can you draw this coordinate grid and mark the coordinates for Ben's quadrilateral after his translation? Label the new coordinates.

2 a Give your partner four coordinates to plot that form a kite.

  b Now translate the kite using your own choice of translation, drawing it in its new position. Ask your partner to work out the translation.

3 Can you translate the coordinates (⁻1,2), (⁻4,6) and (2,⁻3) by $(x + 6, y)$?

···

Going deeper

1 Ben translates his original quadrilateral again. The vertices in the first quadrant end up on points (8,2) and (3,3). What will be the coordinates of the other two vertices?

2 a Can you draw the polygon formed from these coordinates: (3,2), (⁻1,2), (5,⁻1), (⁻3,⁻1)?

  b Can you translate the polygon so that all coordinates are in the fourth quadrant?

  c Can you describe your translation by giving the coordinates of a general point (x,y) after the translation?

Exploring reflections in the four quadrants

Simon draws a pentagon in the 2nd quadrant of a coordinate grid.

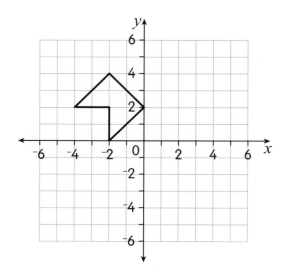

Practice

1 a If Simon wants his pentagon to be in the first quadrant, what axis should he reflect it in?

   b Draw the new position of his pentagon after this transformation.

   c Can you predict what the coordinates would be if he next reflected the pentagon in the x-axis finishing in the third quadrant? Check by drawing the reflection.

2 Can you draw a different pentagon in the fourth quadrant and then reflect it in the x-axis?

3 A square has the coordinates ($^-$3,2), (0,2), (0,$^-$1), ($^-$3,$^-$1). What would be its coordinates after a reflection in the y-axis?

....

Going deeper

1 a If Simon's original pentagon is reflected in the line $x = 1$, what will the coordinates of the new pentagon be?

   b Draw the transformation on your own coordinate grid to check.

2 If Simon reflects his original pentagon and the coordinates of the reflected shape are ($^-$2,$^-$2), (0,$^-$4), ($^-$2,$^-$6), ($^-$4,$^-$4), ($^-$2,$^-$4) in what line has he reflected his shape? Can you explain?

Exploring quadrilaterals on a coordinate grid

Hiromi is making different shapes on a geoboard with axes marked on it.

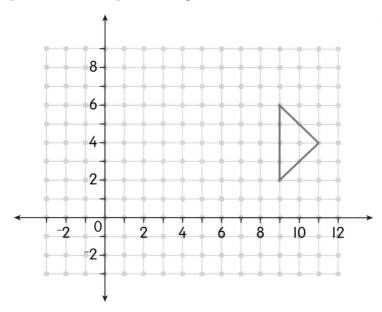

Practice

1 **a** If the vertices of the triangle Hiromi has made remain the same, how can she make a kite by introducing one more vertex?

    b Can you give the coordinates of the fourth vertex to make an inverted kite?

    c Where would the fourth vertex need to go to make a parallelogram?

    d Where would the fourth vertex need to go to make a trapezium?

Going deeper

1 Can you explain where the fourth vertex on Hiromi's geoboard would need to go to make a rhombus?

2 Draw the vertices of three points of a quadrilateral. Ask your partner to place a fourth vertex to make different quadrilaterals and to name them.

Using symbols and letters

1	2	3	4	5	6	7	8	9	10
11	12	13	14	15	16	17	18	19	20
21	22	23	24	25	26	27	28	29	30
31	32	33	34	35	36	37	38	39	40

Practice

1 The number pattern above used 26 as its starting number. Can you describe the rules that connect the other two numbers to the starting number?

2 What happens if you try different starting numbers with this pattern of squares? Can you describe the relationships between all three numbers, using n as the starting number?

3 Can you now write an expression for the total of all three numbers in this pattern, using n as the starting number?

....

Going deeper

1 Using the same pattern of squares as above, can you now write an expression for the total of all three numbers if we call the **smallest** number n?

2 Think about the three-square pattern made by 15, 26 and 37. Can you write a general expression for the total of these numbers using n for the middle number?

3 How does the expression you wrote for **question 2** compare with the one you wrote for practice question 3? Can you explain why?

Generalizing sequences

 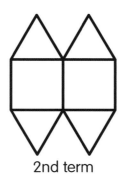

1st term   2nd term

Practice

1 Can you describe the term-to-term rule for the stick pattern above?

2 Can you write a number sentence to calculate the 10th term of this sequence?

3 Can you write a number sentence to calculate the nth term of this sequence?

 4 Design a stick pattern sequence of your own for your partner to work out your term-to-term rule. Can they write number sentences to calculate the 10th and nth terms?

....

Going deeper

1 Can you design a stick pattern sequence in which the number of sticks used in the nth term is $3n + 1$?

2 Can you write an expression for the nth term of the sequence below?

21, 30, 39, 48 …

 3 Can you explain to your partner how you worked out your answer to **question 2**?

Exploring function machines

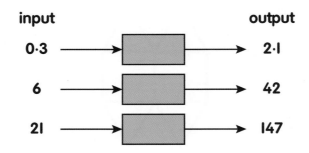

Practice

1 Can you describe what the above function machine is doing?

2 Can you express the relationship between inputs and outputs, using x for input and y for output?

3 Can you express the relationship between inputs and outputs for this function machine, using x for input and y for output?

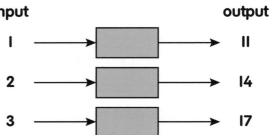

Going deeper

1 If the rule for a function machine is $y = x - 6$, can you say what the input is that gives the output 23?

2 Can you write a general rule for calculating inputs from given outputs of the function machine $y = x - 6$? Write your rule by beginning $x = \ldots$

3 a Here are inputs and related outputs for a new function machine.

Inputs: 3, 4, 5, 6   **Outputs:** 7, 9, 11, 13

Can you express the relation between the inputs and outputs using x for input and y for output?

b Here is a sequence: 3, 5, 7, 9, 11 …

Can you write an expression for the nth term of the sequence? What do you notice? Can you explain?

Rules of arithmetic

$$(3 + 4) + 7 = 7 + 7 = 14$$
$$3 + (4 + 7) = 3 + 11 = 14$$
$$(3 + 7) + 4 = 10 + 4 = 14$$

Practice

1 What do you notice about the three number sentences above? Can you write what you have noticed, in your own words?

2 If $a + b + c = d$, can you write what you have noticed using these letters and brackets?

3 a What do you notice about the three number sentences below?

$$(3 \times 4) \times 7 = 12 \times 7 = 84$$
$$3 \times (4 \times 7) = 3 \times 28 = 84$$
$$(3 \times 7) \times 4 = 21 \times 4 = 84$$

b If $a \times b \times c = d$, can you write what you have noticed using these letters and brackets?

Going deeper

1 a Without calculating, can you explain why $190 + 37 = 200 + 27$?

b Masam says that this will always work because, whatever the numbers,

$$a + b = (a + 10) + (b - 10) = a + 10 + b - 10 = a + b$$

Is he correct? Can you explain why, or why not?

2 Without calculating, can you explain why $145 - 95 = 150 - 100$?

Do you think this will always work? Can you explain using a and b?

3 Given that $\frac{1}{2} + \frac{1}{3} = \frac{3}{6} + \frac{2}{6} = \frac{5}{6}$, can you work out $\frac{1}{a} + \frac{1}{b} = ?$

Glossary

You can find key words that you need here. Other words that you have seen before appear in the glossaries of earlier Pupil Books.

acute angle

An angle smaller than a right angle (90°).
(See also **obtuse angle**, **right angle**.)

average

A 'central' measure used to summarize and represent a set of data with a spread of values.
(See also **mean**.)

BODMAS

Describes the order for tackling multi-operation expressions (Brackets, Orders, Dividing, Multiplying, Adding, Subtracting).

circumference

Distance around a circle.
(See also **diameter**, **radius**.)

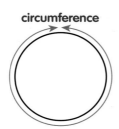

circumference

column method

Written method for adding, subtracting, multiplying or dividing in which numbers are written in columns according to their value.

	2	5	6	7
+	2	3	2	6
	4	8	9	3
			1	

common factor

A whole number that divides into two or more other numbers exactly, e.g. 3 is a common factor of 6, 9 and 12.
(See also **highest common factor**.)

denominator

Lower number of a fraction, gives the fraction its name.
(See also **numerator**, **proper fraction**.)

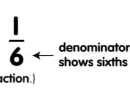

$\dfrac{1}{6}$ ← denominator shows sixths

diameter

The longest distance across a circle, drawn through the centre.
(See also **circumference**, **radius**.)

diameter

equivalent fractions

Fractions of equal value, represented in different ways, e.g. $\frac{1}{4} = \frac{2}{8}$.
(See also **proportion**, **ratio**, **simplifying fractions**.)

highest common factor (HCF)

The highest number that will divide into two or more other numbers exactly, e.g. 12 is the HCF of 24 and 36.
(See also **common factor**, **lowest common multiple**.)

infinite

Without end.

inverse

The reverse or the opposite. Adding and subtracting have an inverse relation to each other and each can undo the other, e.g. 8 + 6 = 14 so 14 − 6 = 8.

long division

Written column method for dividing in which the divisor has two or more digits.
(See also **column method**, **long multiplication**.)

			4	3
2	3	) 9	9	8 0
		9	2	
			7	8
			6	9

long multiplication

Written column method for multiplying in which the multiplier has two or more digits.
(See also **column method**, **long division**.)

		1	2	8
×			1	6
		7₁	6₄	8
1	2	8	0	
2	0	4	8	
	1	1	1	

loss

When something is sold for less than it cost to buy, the 'loss' is the difference between cost and sale price. (See also **profit**).

lowest common multiple (LCM)

The lowest number that is a multiple of two or more other numbers, e.g. the LCM of 3, 4 and 6 is 12. (See also **common factor**, **highest common factor**.)

mean

Mathematical name for an average value used to summarize and represent a set of data with a spread of values.
(See also **average**.)

mixed number

A number written as a whole number and a fraction, e.g. $3\frac{2}{5}$.

net

An arrangement of 2D polygons that can be folded up to make a complete 3D polyhedron.

number rods

Coloured rods of different lengths used for visualizing relationships and calculations.

1 2 3 4 5 6 7 8 9 10

numerator

Upper number of a fraction, shows how many of this kind of fraction.
(See also **denominator, proper fraction**.)

$\frac{3}{6}$ ← **numerator shows that there are 3 sixths**

Numicon Shapes

Shapes of different sizes used for visualizing relationships and calculations.

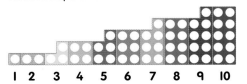

1 2 3 4 5 6 7 8 9 10

obtuse angle

An angle between 90° and 180°.
(See also **acute angle**, **right angle**.)

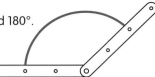

origin

Point where the x-axis and y-axis intersect (0,0).

partitioning

Splitting a number in different ways, usually to help with calculating, e.g. 27 can be partitioned into 2 tens (20) and 7 units (7).

percentage

Used to show a fraction 'out of 100' with the symbol %, e.g. 50%.

perimeter

The distance around a shape.

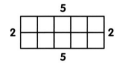

prime factors

The smallest parts a composite number can be divided into, e.g. the prime factors of 12 are 2, 2 and 3, because 2 × 2 × 3 = 12.

product

The number resulting from multiplying two or more numbers together, e.g. in the multiplying calculation 6 × 4 = 24, then 24 is the product.

profit

When something is sold for more than it cost to buy, the difference between what the item cost and what it was sold for is called the 'profit'. (See also **loss**.)

proper fraction

A fraction where the numerator is smaller than the denominator, e.g. $\frac{2}{10}$. (See also **denominator**, **numerator**.)

proportion

An expression that shows two ratios or fractions are equal (in proportion to each other), e.g. $1:2 = 4:8$ or $\frac{1}{2} = \frac{4}{8}$. Also used to express a fraction of a whole, e.g. the proportion of grapes in a bag that are green could be expressed as $\frac{1}{2}$.
(See also **equivalent fractions, ratio, scale factor**.)

quadrant

One of the four equal areas made when a grid, or a shape, is divided into four.

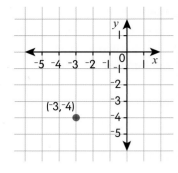

quadrilateral

A polygon with four sides.

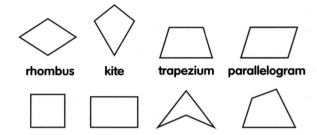

rhombus   kite   trapezium   parallelogram

quotient

The number resulting from dividing one number by another, e.g. in the dividing calculation 24 ÷ 6 = 4, then 4 is the quotient.

radius

A straight line from the centre to the edge of a circle.
(See also **circumference, diameter**.)

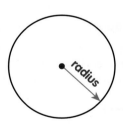

ratio

A way of comparing two or more quantities measured in the same units, e.g. if a is 3 times as much as b this comparison can be written as the ratio $a:b$ is 3:1.
(See also **equivalent fractions, proportion, scale factor**.)

3:1

respectively

In the order given, e.g. 'Emily and Mia are 10 and 11, respectively' means that Emily is 10 and Mia is 11.

right angle

An angle of exactly 90°.
(See also **acute angle, obtuse angle**.)

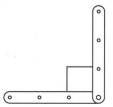

scale factor

Describes the factor by which the length of each side is multiplied when a shape is made larger or smaller in proportion.
(See also **proportion, ratio**.)

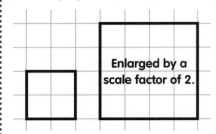

Enlarged by a scale factor of 2.

short written method of multiplying

Written column method for multiplying.
(See also **column method, long division, long multiplication**.)

		2	7	8
×				6
1	6	6	8
			4	4

simplifying fractions

Dividing the numerator and denominator by their highest common factor (HCF) to reduce both to the smallest numbers possible, e.g. $\frac{6}{12} = \frac{1}{2}$, $\frac{8}{24} = \frac{1}{3}$. (See also **highest common factor, lowest common multiple**.)

surface area

The total area of a 3D shape.

transformation

A way of describing the changes that can be made to the size, position, or orientation of a shape or object, e.g. reflection, translation, rotation or scaling.
(See also **translation**.)

translation

A transformation involving sliding a shape or object to a different position in a specific direction.
(See also **transformation**.)

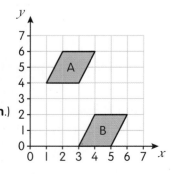

vertex

A point where two sides meet in a flat shape, or a point where three or more edges meet in a 3D shape.